WHY ME?

WHY ME?

REASONING WITH GOD'S SOVEREIGNTY IN THE MIDST OF SUFFERING

KENNETH D. MOORE

Ambassador International
GREENVILLE, SOUTH CAROLINA & BELFAST, NORTHERN IRELAND
www.ambassador-international.com

WHY ME?
Reasoning with God's Sovereignty in the Midst of Suffering

© 2013 by Kenneth D. Moore
All rights reserved

Printed in the United States of America

ISBN: 978-1-62020-203-6
eISBN: 978-1-62020-301-9

Scripture taken from the NEW AMERICAN STANDARD BIBLE®, Copyright © 1960,1962,1963,1968,1971,1972,1973,1975,1977,1995 by The Lockman Foundation. Used by permission.

Cover design: Hannah Stanley
Typesetting: Matthew Mulder
E-book conversion: Anna Riebe

AMBASSADOR INTERNATIONAL
Emerald House
427 Wade Hampton Blvd.
Greenville, SC 29609, USA
www.ambassador-international.com

AMBASSADOR BOOKS
The Mount
2 Woodstock Link
Belfast, BT6 8DD, Northern Ireland, UK
www.ambassadormedia.co.uk

The colophon is a trademark of Ambassador

To Jesus,
Who has carried us along the way
and has blessed us beyond our needs;

to my encouraging wife, Laura,
I am so blessed by your love;

to our precious daughter, Elizabeth,
you are an answer to our prayers;

to our family and friends,
we love you and thank you!

CONTENTS

Introduction	9
CHAPTER 1	
What Dreams Are Made Of	15
CHAPTER 2	
What Happened to My Dreams?	39
CHAPTER 3	
Search Me, O God	67
CHAPTER 4	
Is This on the Map?	83
CHAPTER 5	
Are you the Potter or the Clay?	101
CHAPTER 6	
Stop Today's Mess from Becoming Tomorrow's Mistake	117
CHAPTER 7	
Lord, I Only Have Two Cheeks	137
CHAPTER 8	
I Think I can… I know He will	155
CHAPTER 9	
What a View	167
CHAPTER 10	
Why Me?	189

INTRODUCTION

THE ONLY PENETRATIONS OF THE darkness that night were the flashes of lightning from the coming storm. The once soothing wind increased to a howling winter wind and was soon followed by freezing raindrops. The eerie unsettlement in the pit of my stomach consumed me as I sat in my vehicle in an empty parking lot. I needed to get home if I wanted to get out of the storm, but there was a more dreadful storm that could not be escaped. That very night, a tough meeting occurred that put into motion my dismissal from that pastorate. I felt rejected and ashamed; how could this happen? My head fluttered with thoughts. My mind raced with fears, and the pounding of my heart felt as if it would beat through my chest. I drove around town thinking of the best way to break the news to my wife, and that is how I ended up in an empty parking lot.

Why me? This question was fixated in my mind, and I began to ponder where I was just a few years back. I was serving as pastor in a church where there were some difficulties—more like immovable mountains blocking the path. In my first year of service, three legal issues had to be dealt with in that church. As a single pastor living hours away from the nearest family member, I was overwhelmed. I contacted many godly counselors for suggestions on how to help that church stay open when some were suggesting that the church should close. However, the Lord led that church through tough legal issues, and in the later part of that ministry, God's mighty hand was at work. In my last year at that church, God blessed that church for their faithfulness, and He blessed me with a wife. Days seemed a little brighter, and nights were not filled with as many concerns. Yet, I could sense the Lord's work for me at that church was nearing completion. Six months after marrying Laura, the Lord called us to a community and a church that we anticipated would be home for several years. Our hearts broke as we left behind close friends and her family; however, we anticipated what the Lord had in store for us.

We had so many aspirations for the friendships in the new church and the future renovations for our first home. Unfortunately, those dreams hit a brick wall two years later. The church that called us to serve there voted to force us out of their congregation. We felt like outcasts. Regular activities such as grocery shopping or passing by the church as we went to town were laced with the fear of who we would see and the pain of their rejection. The church family that we served was ripped from our lives. God's calling for me to preach was questioned and doubted by some former church members, and their words played repetitiously in my mind. It was even hard visiting other churches when people knew why I was searching for a new church home. I felt uncomfortable everywhere I went.

There were many times that my anxiety was not in check. I questioned God and felt abandoned by Him at times. A struggle ensued in my heart as I tried to make sense of our situation, and once again, I sought out counsel. We were told to just have faith in God or to think positively about what we had. Others just shrugged off our struggles, telling us that we were not the only couple facing financial or emotional difficulties.

All of their responses have merit to them. We needed to and still need to live by faith. We needed to think positively about what the Lord had blessed us with, but we lived practically as well by thinking about how our bills would be paid. We knew that others suffered greater than we could imagine; yet, what did we need to do in order to deal with our own circumstances?

Although the advice had merit, that does not mean it was beneficial. In fact, I knew all those good truths; so, why did we feel so alone? As you read this, you may be able to identify with these frustrations and with the feeling of isolation. Some of you may even feel as if God is rejecting you. This book is for you! You may be a friend of someone who is struggling with questions concerning God's plan or God's love as troubles in life bombard that individual. You struggle to find encouraging words to say. This book is for you!

The message of this book is to encourage believers that they can praise God and have genuine joy in trials. While there is a tendency to think that escaping trials will be the beginning of praise and joy, the Bible suggests that praise and joy can occur in the midst of pain and suffering.

In order to support this practical optimism of praising God in the midst of struggles, two testimonies were used. The first testimony is one that I often have consulted for assurance and is one of my favorites in the Old Testament. It is from the life of Joseph, which is found in Genesis chapters 37-50. The Bible reveals numerous trials that Joseph faced. Through it all, Joseph concluded that God can use acts caused by malicious intent for His good and the good of His people. You will be able to understand how Joseph came to that conclusion.

The second testimony in this book is mine. Having wrestled with various rejections, I chronicled the journey that led me to praise the Lord in the midst of trials. An emphasis from my testimony will help you identify practical struggles believers face on a daily basis. I felt uncomfortable everywhere I went except for one place: in the arms of God. As I struggled with my insecurities, He drew me into the security of His constant love for me and His continued plan for my life. While I was rejected by a church family, I had to remember that He had already received me into His family. Being my salvation and my Rock, God's work brought stability and peace. I do not have all the answers and have not always responded to God the way He deserves. Yet, He has been gracious to teach me, and I wanted to record an honest and transparent testimony of a believer grappling with questions in life.

Although the desire to imitate the life of Christ is admirable and should be encouraged, trials exist on that journey. Joseph is a fitting example that trials come in various forms. Nonetheless, the greatest trial Joseph faced is the same trial that hinders many believers. The strength from that trial exceeded the combined strength of the aforementioned trials Joseph endured. In essence, Joseph learned which trial provided the greatest resistance to his being the man God had called him to be. This trial serves as the most influential battleground for contemporary believers as well. Identifying this trial is the discussion of the first part of the book.

While progressing on the journey to understanding how believers can praise God in the midst of difficulties, we must explore temptations that can detour that journey. Building upon the premise that all people, not just believers, have trials in life, we must look at possible responses to trials. The second part of this book is critical because going from trials to triumphs in life is usually not a one-step process. Rather, it is a series of decisions based upon solid convictions. You will discover how to identify the differences between the paths that lie ahead. Joseph's testimony provides us the example of the path to choose. I will also share some of my own struggles and failures before following God's path.

The third part of this book offers certain convictions that will help you to have joy in the midst of trials. The story of Joseph is one of hope. The underlining theme emphasized through the life of Joseph is that God is in control. It is remarkable how God used a boy sold into slavery to preserve the life of many, among who are those who sold him into slavery—his brothers. This is sensed in his declaration that what they meant for evil, God meant for good. Joseph did not have to wait for the fulfillment of his dreams to have joy, and neither do you. The testimony concerning Joseph should encourage us that God has a way of turning great trials into greater triumphs.

For me, God demonstrated His peace to us and through our lives while many questions remained unanswered. God provided for us as we waited upon Him. God used us to serve Him when we had little to offer. I cannot adequately put into words the depth of our thankfulness for the presence of God during those dark and lonely times. The strength of His power was channeled into us moment by moment to meet our emotional, physical, and spiritual needs. In the midst of our struggles, God affirmed to us that joy and praise could continue to grow during the storms of life. Our journeys in life will differ, but my prayer is that our destinations are the same, praise God. This journey is not the easiest path to take in life, but it is well worth the trip. I will remind you why God said this journey is worth taking:

> How blessed is the man who finds wisdom
> And the man who gains understanding.
> For her profit is better than the profit of silver
> And her gain better than fine gold.
> She is more precious than jewels;
> And nothing you desire compares with her.
> Long life is in her right hand;
> In her left hand are riches and honor.
> Her ways are pleasant ways
> And all her paths are peace.
> She is a tree of life to those who take hold of her,
> And happy are all who hold her fast.
>
> ~ Proverbs 3:13–18

Chapter 1
WHAT DREAMS ARE MADE OF

PERSECUTION FOR BELIEVING IN THE Lord Jesus Christ and standing upon the truth, God's Word, has been endured by believers since Cain murdered Abel. Undeniably, many examples of fierce persecution have come from religious zealots, and one example was attested by William Bradford. Of the Church of England, he lamented, "Though under many colors & pretences, endeavored to have ye episcopal dignity (after ye popish manner) with their large power & jurisdiction still retained; with all those courts, cannons, & ceremonies, together with all such livings, revenues, & subordinate officers, with other such means as formerly upheld their antichristian greatness, and enabled them with lordly & tyrannous power to persecute ye poor servants of God."[1]

Bradford and other Pilgrims (or Separationists as they were known) found themselves as the target of the Church of England for defying church authority and for betraying England. Both of the charges were linked since the King of England was the leader of the church.

They dreamed of a place where they could freely worship the

---

[1] http://www.pilgrimhall.org/bradfordjournalreligion.htm. Accessed August 15, 2012.

Lord and searched for a place where persecution over doctrine was forbidden. Their journey took them from England to Holland, and finally, to a land that placed three thousand miles of the Atlantic Ocean between them and England. Bradford was one of the 102 people who fought the tough waters of the Atlantic Ocean in order to reach the shore of Plymouth. For the believers, it was their dream to worship God in a place where the only limitation placed on their worship came from the instructions in the Bible.

They began the voyage on September 6, 1620. It was a journey that had no promises for success or some mythical pot of gold at the end of the rainbow. Bradford wrote, "Yea, though they should lose their lives in this action, yet might they have comfort in the same, and their endeavors would be honorable."[2] They were trying to obtain what later was called "The American Dream." When the ships sailed, they had ambitions of a life that surpassed what they left behind. They longed for a brighter future, if not for them, for their children. Bradford's resolve was remarkable because he concluded that even if the voyage failed, the journey was worth taking since their goal was honorable. There was no guarantee of success or a safety net to catch them if they failed; yet, their view of this dream simply sought an opportunity to succeed.

Two months after they set sail, they arrived at Plymouth Rock; upon arrival, they held a prayer service to thank God. Although not their intended destination, the time of the year and their short supply forced them to settle at Plymouth Rock for the winter. With great haste, they built shelters for the winter season, but they were ill prepared to endure the harsh winter conditions after enduring

---

2 http://www.pilgrimhall.org/bradfordjournalemigrate.htm. Accessed August 15, 2012.

two months on a turbulent ocean. Unfortunately, nearly half of the Pilgrims died during the winter months that year. In the spring of 1621, Samoset, a Native American, approached the Pilgrims and greeted them in their language, one that he learned from English fishermen and traders. Samoset introduced the Pilgrims to another Indian named Squanto, who taught the Pilgrims how to live off the land in the New World.

The Pilgrims told Samoset about Jesus Christ, and he became a believer. Having been introduced to peace with God through Jesus Christ, Samoset assumed a vital role in the signing of a long-lasting peace treaty between the Pilgrims and the Wampanoag Indians. The harvest of 1621 was very good for the Pilgrims, and they were thankful for the friendly Native Americans as well. Thus, a three-day feast was set aside for the Pilgrims and the Native Americans to give thanks. The celebration came when they did not know if they would be able to endure another harsh winter, but they made it a priority to thank God anyway.

The goal of this book is to motivate you to pursue God's plan for His people to live with true joy, peace, and praise even in the midst of difficulties. I am not going to pacify you by telling you that this journey is really not that tough, because it is. In fact, you will discover a biblical pattern that has allowed believers to do the unthinkable and the unnatural. If you accept this challenge, God will reveal to you a way that will keep you from fearing the unknown or failing to walk with Him. You will find a joyous faith that will not waver in trials; rather, it will be resolute despite trials. If you accept this challenge, your confidence in His plan will be stronger during the storms of doubt and confusion, since there is a peace that passes all understanding. If you accept this challenge, you will learn how to experience joyful praise in the midst of hardship. Ability to praise God in the midst of difficulties, and being chosen to experience those difficulties, is a beautiful portrait of God's work. For in that praise, God becomes our true joy and peace. The journey is hard, but the destination is beneficial.

Since the premise of this book encourages believers to wholeheartedly follow God's plan, this chapter begins with an examination of His plan and the pains God endured to accomplish His plan. Then, we will examine expectations God has of His people. The commitment to follow God's plan requires a biblically founded conviction that directs attitudes and actions. This chapter will help you to identify the right dream that God has for you and decide whether you are willing to pursue that dream.

WHAT DOES GOD ENVISION FOR HIS PEOPLE?

God's plan for His people goes back to the beginning. Adam and Eve were the centerpieces of God's creation as evidenced on the sixth day of creation when God said, "Let Us make man in Our image, according to Our likeness."[3] So, what does it mean that God made man in His image and likeness? Within one statement, God summarized how the purpose of creation was to have a people who would duplicate His character and represent His decrees.

First, God envisioned a people who would enjoy a personal relationship with Him. Consider the fact that before making man, God created. The word "create" emphasizes that out of nothing, God simply spoke creation into existence. According to Genesis 1:3, 6, 9, 11, 14, 15, 20, 24, the heavens, the earth, angelic beings,

---

3   Genesis 1:26a; All Scripture will come from the New American Standard Version unless otherwise noted.

land, water, vegetation, and every living creature were created just by the spoken command of God. There was no need of floating particles to collide or for millions or billions of years to allow evolution the time necessary for humans to exist. There was no lapse of time for the command of God to be transmitted; when God spoke, there was an immediate result. For example, when He commanded there to be light, there was light. Before God spoke, there was no light; furthermore, God has no need for light. On the contrary, man needs light, and for man's purpose and blessing, God created light instantly.

    The marvel of God creating out of nothing is surpassed only by the elevated status God granted by making man. God could have created man with a spoken word, but God distinguished man from the rest of creation. God took the matter and time that He created and personally made man special. Concerning the thought of God's personal touch, the psalmist wrote, "For You formed my inward parts; You wove me in my mother's womb."[4] When my wife, Laura, found out that she was pregnant, we celebrated. Similar to many first time parents, we saved everything, including the picture from the first ultrasound, and we gazed upon that picture often for the next few months. Over the duration of her pregnancy, technology enabled us to view the development of that small person within the womb of my wife; therefore, we looked forward to the visits with the doctor. There was no doubt that God allowed us to see a part of His creative work; with great awe, we learned of Elizabeth's development and had a great wonder concerning God's work. We greatly anticipated the day we would meet our daughter, who was formed by God; on May 23, 2012, that bundle of joy was born. Although

---

4   Psalm 139:13.

we saw glimpses of her personality even in the first few months, the coming moments that God has allotted us to watch her grow will reveal the person God formed in my wife's womb.

The psalmist probed deeper into God's magnificence when he wrote, "My frame was not hidden from You, when I was made in secret, and skillfully wrought in the depths of the earth; Your eyes have seen my unformed substance; and in Your book were all written the days that were ordained for me, when as yet there was not one of them."[5] These verses add to the wonder of God's work since God intimately knew my daughter before my wife and I conceived her. It was in the "depths of the earth" that God knew Elizabeth to the smallest detail—even to the number of days she has on this earth. The psalmist identified that God has a deliberate plan in forming people in their mothers' wombs. God envisioned a people who would enjoy a personal relationship with Him.

What does it mean that God made man in His image and likeness? In addition to creating a people who would enjoy a personal relationship with Him, God envisioned a people who would reason with His knowledge and wisdom. Do not neglect or underestimate God's knowledge by claiming it is limited to "just spiritual talk"; God is the source of all accurate knowledge. This includes but is not limited to the fields of scientific, mathematical, philosophical, and psychiatric studies. According to Job chapters 38–41, God asserted having a complete knowledge of all constellations in the heavens, including the precise mathematical dimensions in the heavens; the complexities of the earth's climate; and the intricate characteristics of the animal kingdom. Job chapters 3–37 deal with tough questions concerning why God allows difficulties to affect believers.

---

5   Psalm 139:15–16.

Numerous questions within those chapters are similar to questions people have today about suffering and sickness. God's monologue in Job chapters 38–41 is impressive and interesting when He challenged Job with questions of His own. God evidenced the vastness of His knowledge; fields of science, medicine, math, and astrology served to display that God's knowledge goes well beyond "just spiritual talk."

Studying the subjects in the previous paragraph is not the only way to lead one to appreciate God. God's grace has been given to humanity as attested by their ability to reason, to think logically, and to learn about various subjects. It is an honor to study various subjects in order to discover a portion of God's limitless knowledge, and it is beneficial to other people to study various subjects. Thus, God made man with the capability to think critically by assessing a problem and ascertaining possible ways to best find a solution.

Imagine a disease that could affect an estimated sixty percent of the world's population and kill twenty percent of the world's population. During the eighteenth century, that dreaded disease was smallpox.

In the late eighteenth century, Benjamin Jetsy, a Dorset farmer, and Edward Jenner, an English country doctor, made an enlightened discovery. While smallpox affected most of the population, it was observed that dairy workers who had recovered from cowpox, a much lesser disease than smallpox, were immune to smallpox. In the midst of a smallpox epidemic, Jetsy removed pus from a cowpox blister and infected his wife and children. Although they developed cowpox, they never contracted smallpox. As for Jenner, he learned of Jetsy's experiment and other studies with similar conclusions, and he took pus from cowpox blisters from one patient and inoculated the pus into an eight-year-old boy named James Phipps. Later, Jenner injected the pus from smallpox blisters into Phipps. Although he had cowpox, he was never affected by the deadly disease. The usage of a live virus as a vaccine is still used today. As a result, other vaccines have been successful in the treatment of polio, measles, and of course smallpox, just to name a few. God made man with the ability to assess problems, to learn about possible solutions, and to implement their conclusions.

God made man in His image and likeness, envisioning a people who would represent His character in front of all creation. God personally communicated with Adam and Eve and gave them the ability to reason with His knowledge; thus, God made man stewards over creation. God said, "Let them rule over the fish of the sea and over the birds of the sky and over the cattle and over all the earth, and over every creeping thing that creeps on the earth."[6]

The purpose was to provide a way for man to demonstrate His knowledge of God; therefore, He made them stewards over His creation to promote order and righteousness in the manner that He would have done. They were commissioned to rule over creation with the same principles and heart that the Lord displayed to them. They were to imitate God's character to creation; in other words, man was God's ambassador to all creation. Reverence for God's commands and an imitation of God's character were expressions of worship Adam and Eve enjoyed.

Since the beginning, God has not changed His mind or His expectation of having people imitate His character and announce His decrees to others. In the perfect Garden, they had the responsibility to care for God's creation, to cultivate the fields of the earth,

---

6 Genesis 1:26b.

to display the essence of a loving relationship, and to fill the earth with people who love Him. However, there was a change in the Garden, a drastic change that would taint the perfection of God's work—as well as serve as the means for God to reveal another part of His glorious plan.

WHAT DOES GOD ENDURE ON BEHALF OF HIS PEOPLE?

Toys are everywhere in our house. We have toys that roll, toys that have pieces that fit together, and toys that make the most annoying sounds ever heard by the human ear. Those are just the toys that are in the house; we have toys boxed up in closets and in my shed, ugh! We have enough toys—or so I think. Yet, there are times when a child sees another child playing with a toy and it turns out to be the same exact toy the first child wants. There is a nature, even within the heart of those "little angels," that screams, "I want it; it is mine!" Children are not the only ones guilty of screaming for what they want, and the twenty-first century is not the first time selfishness has been displayed.

Adam and Eve lived in a utopia environment! They had peace with God and with each other. They were not afraid of snakes, spiders, or any animal for that matter; they lived and ruled in a world that was not dominated by fear. God was their best friend, and the world was in their hands, literally! The only forbiddance to Adam and Eve was the fruit from one tree in the Garden. Simple enough, they had at their disposal the fruit from every other tree and the food that grew from plants. God did not forbid one region of trees in the Garden, nor did He forbid one type of trees in the Garden; simply, God commanded them not to eat from one tree. He warned them that if they ate of that fruit, "in the day that you eat from it you will surely die."⁷ On one hand, they could have all the food that the world had to offer and live; on the other hand, they could eat from one forbidden tree and die. Nonetheless, they ate the fruit from the forbidden tree. With one rebellious act, they sacrificed personal and satisfactory fellowship with God, and peace with the animal kingdom and each other for one bite of forbidden fruit. After they sinned, God walked through the Garden, and they attempted to hide from Him. For the first time, Adam and Eve experience fear, and they feared God. Their utopia ended.

Why did they disregard God's command? The tempter persuaded Eve to believe that "You surely will not die! For God knows that in the day you eat from it your eyes will be opened, and you will be like God, knowing good and evil."⁸ The real reason Adam and Eve ate the fruit was that they believed God held back blessings, and they wanted to be like Him; they wanted to be on His level. Foolishly, they believed equality with God was their right and in their grasp.

Not only did they realize that equality with God is impossible, but they paid a deep price for their rebellion. Man's personal relationship with God was destroyed, and man's reasoning with God's knowledge became filled with delusional thoughts; thus, man's responsibility to represent God became defective. Simply put, the image and likeness of God, that described man's privilege according to Genesis 1:26, was tainted from that moment of rebellion. Unfortunately, their sin against God corrupted humanity and set an example of defiance for creation to witness.

---

7   Genesis 2:17.

8   Genesis 3:4b–5.

Since then, all people have evidenced their sin nature by doing what comes naturally to them: sinning.

God has endured years of constant rebellion Since the Fall in the Garden. The image of God that signifies man's significance has been trampled upon and ridiculed. Paul lamented,

> For since the creation of the world His invisible attributes, His eternal power and divine nature, have been clearly seen, being understood through what has been made, so that they are without excuse. For even though they knew God, they did not honor Him as God or give thanks, but they became futile in their speculations, and their foolish heart was darkened. Professing to be wise, they became fools, and exchanged the glory of the incorruptible God for an image in the form of corruptible man and of birds and four-footed animals and crawling creatures. Therefore God gave them over in the lusts of their hearts to impurity, so that their bodies would be dishonored among them. For they exchanged the truth of God for a lie, and worshipped and served the creature rather than the Creator, who is blessed forever. Amen. For this reason God gave them over to degrading passions; for their women exchanged the natural function for that which is unnatural, and in the same way also the men abandoned the natural function of the woman and burned in their desire toward one another, men with men committing indecent acts and receiving in their own persons the due penalty of their error. And just as they did not see fit to acknowledge God any longer, God gave them over to a depraved mind, to

do those things which are not proper, being filled with all unrighteousness, wickedness, greed, evil; full of envy, murder, strife, deceit, malice; they are gossips, slanderers, haters of God, insolent, arrogant, boastful, inventors of evil, disobedient to parents, without understanding, untrustworthy, unloving, unmerciful; and although they know the ordinance of God, that those who practice such things are worthy of death, they not only do the same, but also give hearty approval to those who practice them.[9]

Clearly, Paul described sin as a willful insurrection toward God with mankind deliberately substituting worship that should be only toward their Creator, joyfully worshiping the creation instead. This was not an innocent mistake of eating from the wrong tree by Adam and Eve. They knew the seriousness of their violation, and that was the reason they attempted to hide from God. By knowing Him as intimately as they did, they knew God's fury against those who chose to defy Him.

The tempter, better known as Satan, expressed the same defiant spirit when he expressed his dissatisfaction with serving God. Leading one-third of the angelic beings, Satan rebelled against God because he thought he deserved to be served by God. He wanted to have a throne controlling creation. He wanted to be praised by creation for his beauty and power, but his rebellion led to his being kicked out of heaven, and immediately Satan and the rest of his coconspirators were judged with no possibility to repent.

Unlike the penalty meted out to Satan and his followers, God's messengers warned people that their sin was an abomination to Him

---

[9] Romans 1:20–32.

and gave them opportunities to repent. It is written, "How lovely on the mountains are the feet of him who brings good news, who announces peace and brings good news of happiness, who announces salvation, and says to Zion, 'Your God reigns!'"[10] Beginning with Abel, God has sent numerous messengers proclaiming His truth. They boldly confronted kings and kingdoms, comforted the faithful ones in the midst of misery, and provided a correct view of God to idolaters. Unlike the judgment given to Satan and the rebellious angels, the messengers brought a message of hope. Jeremiah attested, "For I know the plans that I have for you, declares the Lord, plans for welfare and not for calamity to give you a future and a hope."[11] These messengers called people to forsake their idols, to repent of their wicked ways so that they would seek the Lord and follow His righteous ways wholeheartedly.

The power to change a heart is impossible with man; therefore, God graciously sent messengers so that He could display His power to the people. They were messengers who lived "by faith" and witnesses to the mighty power of God. By faith, they "conquered kingdoms, performed acts of righteousness, obtained promises, shut the mouths of lions, quenched the power of fire, escaped the edge of the sword, from weakness were made strong, became mighty in war, put foreign armies to flight."[12] These examples of power were to validate that God sent the messengers and so that the people would have a testimony to witness what God can do. Whenever God performed these examples, He reminded the leaders and the

---

10 Isaiah 52:7.

11 Jeremiah 29:11.

12 Hebrews 11:33–34.

people to give Him praise so that their security would rest in Him instead of resting in their leaders or themselves. Nevertheless, many of these messengers endured great hardships. It is written, "They were stoned, they were sawn in two, they were tempted, they were put to death with the sword; they went about in sheepskins, in goatskins, being destitute, afflicted, ill-treated (men of whom the world was not worthy), wandering in deserts and mountains and caves and holes in the ground."[13]

Nonetheless, God stayed committed to sending His message so that the word of repentance would be presented to people. Since people mistreated the prophets who testified of a Messiah able to redeem people, God sent the Messiah, the Lord Jesus Christ. He is the Alpha and Omega, the Bright Morningstar, the Lion of Judah, the Prince of peace, the seed of David, the Anointed One, the King of kings, and He is the Lord of lords. He is also "the image of the invisible God, the firstborn of all creation. For by Him all things were created, both in the heavens and on earth, visible and invisible, whether thrones or dominions or rulers or authorities—all things have been created through Him and for Him. He is before all things, and in Him all things hold together"[14]

Jesus spoke like no one else. He astonished crowds with His teaching; even in His hometown, people were amazed. Jesus had not received the formal education that the Pharisees had, and He never studied under Gamaliel such as the Apostle Paul did. Nevertheless, Jesus baffled the educated with His knowledge. Furthermore, Jesus performed miracles like no one else.

---

13 Hebrews 11:37–38.

14 Colossians 1:15–17.

His disciples witnessed the immediate calming of such a dreadful storm that these skilled fishermen thought they were going to perish. When the disciples of John the Baptist were sent on behalf of John to reaffirm that Jesus was the Messiah, He answered, "Go and report to John what you hear and see: the blind receive sight and the lame walk, the lepers are cleansed and the deaf hear, the dead are raised up, and the poor have the gospel preached to them. And blessed is he who does not take offense at Me."[15] But some did take offense at Him; for example, when He fed the multitudes with five loaves and two fish, the crowd offered to follow Him if He continued to give them bread. Knowing they had wrong motives, Jesus talked about the commitment to be His disciple. It is written, "As of a result of this many of His disciples withdrew and were not walking with Him anymore."[16]

Jesus was not the leader of a circus, desiring merely to entertain people or be a puppet under their control. He came as the "the image of the invisible God, the firstborn of all creation." As to the image, Jesus came to perfectly demonstrate the totality of God's exact nature. He is the only absolute and accurate description of God. Concerning Jesus being the firstborn of all creation, it does not mean that Jesus was created. Since Paul clarified that point by writing, "For by Him all things were created"; then, how does firstborn relate to Christ? The word *firstborn* also refers to one who has the primary rank or the one who is in charge. In other words, Jesus came to give man the means by which he can have a right relationship with God. Jesus came so that the minds of believers can be transformed, renewed, and conformed so that

---

15 Matthew 11:4–6.

16 John 6:66.

man can correctly reason with God's knowledge. Jesus came so that believers can represent God truthfully.

The work of Jesus should have been received with gratitude and thankfulness, but He was despised, rejected, and crucified. Speaking to man's rejection of His work, Jesus said, "This is the judgment, that the Light has come into the world, and men loved the darkness rather than the Light, for their deeds were evil."[17] Humans are not only involved in sinful activities but are also infatuated by their sinful activities. Besides breaking God's law repetitiously and rejecting God's grace, they also embrace and enhance their rebellion.

God has endured countless accusations suggesting that sometimes sin goes unpunished. These accusations pierce to the heart of God's ability to judge righteously. Biblical history provides many examples of prideful rebellion against the ways of God; there have been others who have thought their sin does not matter, and others who believe they have been so secretive that nobody knows their wickedness. Even God's servants have been perplexed that God allows wicked men to live without judgment. For example, Habakkuk cried out, "How long, O Lord, will I call for help, and You will not hear? I cry out to You, "Violence!" yet You do not save. Why do You make me see iniquity, and cause me to look on wickedness? Yes, destruction and violence are before me; strife exists and contention arises. Therefore the law is ignored and justice is never upheld. For the wicked surround the righteous; therefore justice comes out perverted." [18]

Before the throne of God, John testified of believers who are martyrs as saying, "How long, O Lord, holy and true, will

---

17   John 3:19.

18   Habakkuk 1:2–4.

you refrain from judging and avenging our blood on those who dwell on the earth?"[19] It was observed, "Furthermore, I have seen under the sun that in the place of justice there is wickedness and in the place of righteousness there is wickedness."[20] God accused Israel, "So now we call the arrogant blessed; not only are the doers of wickedness built up but they also test God and escape."[21] Some people believe they can defy the commands of God and escape His wrath.

Although God has endured man's rebellion, He will not endure it forever. God promised, "I will vindicate the holiness of My great name which has been profaned among the nations, which you have profaned in their midst. Then the nations will know that I am the Lord," declares the Lord God, "when I prove Myself holy among you in their sight."[22] God has determined a day when all rebellion will be judged. Paul emphasized the graciousness of God should not be confused with a negligence to deal with man's rebellion. Paul clarified, "For the wrath of God is revealed from heaven against all ungodliness and unrighteousness of men who suppress the truth in unrighteousness, because that which is known about God is evident within them; for God made it evident to them."[23] Although we know not the year, month, or even the day when God will judge man's rebellion against Him, the fact that rebellion will be severely judged is

---

19   Revelation 6:10.
20   Ecclesiastes 3:16.
21   Malachi 3:15.
22   Ezekiel 36:23.
23   Romans 1:18–19.

guaranteed. A lesson needs to be learned from the days of Noah; God said, "My Spirit shall not strive with man forever, because he also is flesh."[24]

WHAT DID GOD ESTABLISH FOR HIS PEOPLE?

On the night of the Lord's betrayal, He went to the Garden of Gethsemane to pray with His disciples. In the midst of the night, light from many torches could be seen as the rebellious mob carrying swords and clubs was led by the traitor, Judas Iscariot. He led the large mob of chief priests and elders with Roman soldiers to find Jesus. Judas betrayed the Messiah with a kiss, and Jesus was seized and taken into custody. Immediately, one of the disciples, Peter, lunged forward with his drawn sword and cut the ear off the slave of the high priest.

On this particular night, faced with a traitor, an angry mob, and lying priests and elders, who did Jesus rebuke? Rebuking Peter, He said, "Do you think that I cannot appeal to My Father, and He will at once put at My disposal more than twelve legions of angels?"[25] Jesus had the opportunity and the right to command at least twelve legions of angels to eliminate that mob, but He did not.

The reason that Jesus did not summon them is found in the following verse. Jesus continued, "How then will the Scriptures be fulfilled, which say that it must happen this way? ... But all this has taken place to fulfill the Scriptures of the prophets."[26] The prophet Isaiah eloquently described the redemptive plan of God with these

---

24 Genesis 6:3.

25 Matthew 26:53.

26 Matthew 26:54, 56.

words, "But the Lord was pleased to crush Him, putting Him to grief; if He would render Himself as a guilt offering, He will see His offspring, He will prolong His days, and the good pleasure of the Lord will prosper in His hand."[27]

God enforced the price for sin. In the Garden, God warned Adam, "From any tree of the garden you may eat freely; but from the tree of the knowledge of good and evil you shall not eat, for in the day that you eat from it you will surely die."[28] To Ezekiel, God said, "The person who sins will die."[29] Lest anyone think himself to be without sin, Paul proclaimed, "For all have sinned and fall short of the glory of God."[30] Then, Paul continued the indictment, "For the wages of sin is death."[31] The seriousness of sin cannot be underestimated when seen from God's perspective, for He has clearly and repetitiously proclaimed sin to be an abomination to His nature. Therefore, He proclaimed that all sin would be judged harshly. Lest anyone conclude that the holiness of God and the wrath of God cannot coexist with the love of God and the mercy of God, the cross—as horrific as it was—displayed the beauty of God's love and mercy perfectly. Jesus Christ was not guilty of any sin; He was just and pure in the eyes of God. He willingly came because He knew that man could never be righteous without His intervention.

To all those who believe they can escape God's wrath, the only evidence they need is the cross. The nonchalant attitude that mocks

---

27 Isaiah 53:10.

28 Genesis 2:16–17.

29 Ezekiel 18:20.

30 Romans 3:23.

31 Romans 6:23a.

the existence or the extent of God's wrath needs to take a serious evaluation of the crucifixion. Isaiah established that it was God the Father engineering the road to the cross. Yes, the Roman soldiers drove the nails into Jesus' feet and hands; yes, it was the Jewish elders who provided false accusations against Jesus; yes, it was Judas who betrayed Jesus. They are responsible for their actions; yet, Isaiah said that the Lord crushed Jesus. The Lord was in charge the whole time and accomplished His purpose by crushing His innocent Son. Since God carried out His wrath on a willing Son, what makes people think that God would withhold judgment from the guilty?

What was God doing by crushing Jesus? First, God exhibited the payment for sin. Appreciation for the sacrifice of Jesus heightens when a proper understanding of the guilt offering is known. As it says in Isaiah, "If He would render Himself as a guilt offering." The guilt offering served two purposes. First, the guilt offering was given for sins that the person unintentionally committed or was unaware of. From God's perspective, all sin—intentional or unintentional, known or unknown—is offensive to His nature. Ignorance of God's law is no excuse for the lawbreaker since all sin is known by God; thus, He cannot ignore the sin. All sin must be judged harshly. Imagine for just a moment that man could make restitution for himself (which no person can ever do!); how does man remember, much less know, every sin he committed? It is impossible for man to recount every sin committed during an entire lifetime, and that is why Jesus died! It has been rightly said that Jesus paid a debt that He did not owe because we had a debt we could not pay. It is worse than that because Jesus paid a debt so deep that we have no clue how much we truly owed.

It has been rightly said that Jesus paid a debt that He did not owe because we had a debt we could not pay. It is worse than that because Jesus paid a debt so deep that we have no clue how much we truly owed. The guilt offering required for the victim to receive in full everything lost plus an additional twenty percent. For example, a thief who stole $100 had to return $100 plus an additional $20 to the victim. If it is hard to keep count of every sin, known and unknown alike, try making a complete and additional restitution for those sins. In essence, man would be required to return to God all the praise, worship, and obedience due to Him as if sin never corrupted His creation. Does that make you feel overwhelmed? It should; in fact, you should feel hopeless to ever think that the honor to be in God's presence can be achieved by the works of man. God exhibited the steep price of sin when Christ was crucified on the cross.

Secondly, by crushing Jesus, God established permanent redemption through the sacrifice of His Lamb. The road of redemption was paved and paid for by the blood of God's sacrifice, Jesus Christ. Because of that sacrifice, Paul rejoiced that believers "have put on the new self who is being renewed to a true knowledge according to the image of the One who created him."[32] Through sin, the image in which God made man was severely damaged; through salvation, Christ restored that image. He bridged the gap between God and man in order for man to fulfill the purpose of being made in the image and likeness of God. Specifically, Christ is the way for one to have a relationship with God as attested by giving man a new self. The new self is the new creation made alive by the Holy Spirit, and He renews the mind of a believer in order to reason with God's knowledge. Notice how Paul linked the renewed mind, which

---

32 Colossians 3:10.

has the capability to understand true knowledge, and the image of Christ. Next, through the renewing of the mind, the believer is able to represent God in a way that glorifies Him, and that road of redemption is what God established through Jesus Christ.

God's work is amazing! What adds to that amazement is that God's plan was not formulated as a response to sin in the Garden; God's plan was formulated before Adam and Eve were made. Paul emphasized, "For those whom He foreknew, He also predestined to become conformed to the image of His Son, so that He would be the firstborn among many brethren; and these who He predestined, He also called; and these whom He called, He also justified; and these whom He justified, He also glorified."[33] From even before the foundations of the heavens and the earth, God's plan has always been to redeem a people unto His holiness and to display His power through salvation. That has been God's plan, is God's plan, and will be God's plan unto Judgment Day.

God made man to have a personal relationship with Him, reason with Him, and represent Him. If the reader grasps this concept, you see trials through a different lens and life through a different perspective. Every trial God allows and every blessing that God gives is saturated with a focus on making believers more in His image.

Your walk with God will be filled with anger, frustration, and confusion if you do not understand God's plan to make you in His image and likeness. On the contrary, a believer who willingly embraces God's plan and who wholeheartedly trusts God during the journey will be blessed beyond measure. There will be a new joy, peace, power, and pleasure that can only be given by God and in

---

33 Romans 8:29–30.

any circumstance. Commit your heart to Him to walk you to the destination that God envisioned for you, endured hardships for you, and established for you. What does this journey look like? The next two chapters display ways that God can sanctify His people just as He did in the life of Joseph.

Chapter 2

WHAT HAPPENED TO MY DREAMS?

THE FIRST CHRISTIAN BOOK I read, outside the Bible, was the classical book called *The Pilgrim's Progress*. I was a young boy with a vast imagination, and the narrative story written by John Bunyan intrigued my young mind. The plot was the journey of the main character, Christian, and his journey from the City of Destruction to the Celestial City. Christian encountered places such as the Slough of Despond and people such as Mr. Worldly Wiseman who proposed alternatives to making the journey to the Celestial City. Along the way, though, characters named Evangelist and Help provided much needed direction and encouragement. This allegory has done more than provide leisure reading; it has also encouraged many generations to faithfully pursue the journey God has called believers to walk. For Bunyan though, *The Pilgrim's Progress* was more than just a novel; it was the testimony of struggles for the believer with which Bunyan was all too familiar.

Under Charles II, those who were Nonconformists and Presbyterians endured persecution since all citizens were required to attend their Anglican parish church. Furthermore, it was against the law to conduct a religious service except if it was conducted according to the policy of the Anglican Church. From 1660-1672, Bunyan spent much time in jail with a few intervals of freedom because of his refusal to quit preaching the gospel at Nonconformist meetings. He was offered freedom on various occasions, provided he would stop preaching at the Nonconformist meetings; he replied, "If you let me out today, I will preach again tomorrow."[34]

The greatest hardship on John Bunyan focused on his family. After his first wife died in 1658, he married again in 1660, which is the same year his imprisonments began. His second wife had to care for four children, one of whom was blind. Although he made tagged shoelaces while in prison to support his family, his heart ached greatly for them and for the financial stress placed upon them due to his imprisonments. There were two books in his possession while in jail that provided much needed instruction and encouragement; they were *John Foxe's Book of Martyrs* and the Bible. Within the pages of those books, John Bunyan read many accounts of believers who suffered greatly for following God's ways. Their testimonies and God's Word inspired Bunyan, who wrote tracts, pamphlets, and his masterpiece, *The Pilgrim's Progress,* from the confines of prison. Despite the horrific conditions of the prison and the alienation from his family, God used John Bunyan in a way that influences people years beyond Bunyan's life, in places where Bunyan never visited.

The Bible assures believers that "God causes all things to work together for good to those who love God, to those who are called according to His purpose."[35] John Bunyan and the main character of

---

34   Harold J. Chadwick, *The New Foxe's Book of Martyrs* (North Brunswick, NJ: Bridge-Logos, 1997), 312.

35   Romans 8:28.

this book, Joseph, are examples of how God can take dire circumstances and use them for good and for His glory.

Concerning Joseph, the glorious destination envisioned by God began with turbulent conditions. As it is written, "His brothers saw that their father loved him more than all his brothers; and so they hated him and could not speak to him on friendly terms."[36] Their hatred of Joseph did not stem merely from one event or misunderstanding. The brothers directed a deep-seated, bitter spirit toward Joseph. They simply could not give him even a friendly greeting such as "hello" or "have a nice day." They wished him no good; in fact, they despised everything about Joseph.

The first reason for their animosity was favoritism, which plagued the family lines through generations. Joseph's grandmother, Rebekah, had favored Jacob more than Esau, while Isaac, Joseph's grandfather, had favored Esau. Wanting to give Esau a blessing, which was highly regarded, Isaac asked Esau to fix him a meal from a hunt. Overhearing the request, Rebekah instructed Jacob to disguise himself as Esau; thus, Isaac unknowingly stole Esau's blessing. Jacob continued the trend of favoritism through his marriage to Leah and Rachel, "Now the Lord saw that Leah was unloved, and He opened her womb, but Rachel was barren."[37] There was no hiding Jacob's love for Rachel; Jacob worked seven years for Laban, Rachel's father, for the right to have her hand in marriage. Upon the completion of seven years, Laban gave Leah in marriage to Jacob. Although irate, Jacob agreed to work another seven years in order to marry his true love, Rachel. Time did not change Jacob's favoritism, nor did it heal wounds, as

---

36 Genesis 37:4.

37 Genesis 29:31.

demonstrated when Jacob loved Rachel more than he loved Leah; then, he loved the son of his favorite wife more than he loved his other children.

The second reason for the brothers' animosity was that Jacob gave Joseph an unparalleled trust. The custom of the day dictated that the oldest son would receive the greatest portion of a father's inheritance and would be the most influential among the siblings. Yet Joseph, who was younger than they were, garnered the prestige and power from Jacob. When Joseph was sent to shepherd part of Jacob's flock with the sons of Jacob's concubines, he brought back a bad report about them. The Hebrew word for "bad report" (*dibbah*) can refer to slandering or defaming someone with an evil intent, but it is also used when a truthful report is bad news, such as the report of the ten spies in Numbers 13:32. Joseph's truthfulness was not questioned in these verses by Jacob, and the brothers learned that Joseph would not ignore their wicked ways.

To demonstrate his love and special treatment, Jacob gave Joseph a varicolored tunic. This garment is known to have extended to the ankles and wrists. A working man wore a shorter garment so that he could work, but a longer tunic would be too restraining. Longer tunics were worn by those who did not have to work manually; thus, this tunic symbolized prestige and privilege. Although it is uncertain whether the bad report given by Joseph had any impact on receiving the tunic, it is interesting that the tunic was given after the report. Possibly, the coat could have signified Jacob's lack of trust in his other sons, but it definitely signified that Joseph was Jacob's favorite. Despite the tradition of the eldest son receiving most of the father's inheritance, Joseph seemed likely to receive the lion's share.

For the brothers, the news went from bad to worse. Genesis 37 describes a young Joseph who received two separate dreams. Telling the brothers of the first dream, Joseph said, "Behold, we were binding sheaves in the field, and lo, my sheaf rose up and also stood erect; and behold, your sheaves gathered around and bowed to my sheaf."[38] Likewise, in the second dream, Joseph said, "The sun and the moon and eleven stars were bowing down to me."[39] In other words, Joseph would be their superior before Jacob died. If true, the dreams emphatically meant that they would be inferior to Joseph sooner than anticipated; in addition, if these dreams were true, the source had to be God. Therefore, God was added to the list of those who favored Joseph above the rest of them.

Since they had been unwilling to speak kindly to Joseph before the dreams, their hatred intensified after the dreams.

THE TRIAL OF CONSPIRACY

What ingredients constitute a conspiracy? Writing to brokenhearted and discouraged sojourners, James gave practical advice so that they would persevere in their walk with Christ. These believers were chased from their homes and possibly alienated from their families due to their faith in Christ. Their pursuers were religious people who conspired to stop anyone talking about—much less believing in—Jesus Christ. James explained to these believers why practicing "believers" had such contempt for them. Yet, it was another group—teachers within the church—who demonstrated their contempt for these believers through secretive conspiracies. James wrote,

---

38 Genesis 37:7.

39 Genesis 37:9.

> Who among you is wise and understanding? Let him show by his good behavior his deeds in the gentleness of wisdom. But if you have bitter jealousy and selfish ambition in your heart, do not be arrogant and so lie against the truth. This wisdom is not that which comes down from above, but is earthly, natural, demonic. For where jealousy and selfish ambition exist, there is disorder and every evil thing. But the wisdom from above is first pure, then peaceable, gentle, reasonable, full of mercy and good fruits, unwavering, without hypocrisy.[40]

This passage provides insight concerning the methods and motives for a conspiracy, which perfectly corresponds to the story of Joseph.

Concerning the methods of the conspirators, James began with "bitter jealousy," which conveys a harsh envy resulting in promotion of one's idea to the exclusion of others. These conspiring teachers sought control and ways to maintain control over "their church." They felt threatened by anyone who thought differently than they. In essence, the devious teachers wanted the church to become dependent upon them. From their perspective, no need existed for another viewpoint to be expressed or respected in the church, especially perspectives contrary to their own. They were the leaders, and they demanded to conduct the church as they saw fit without being questioned.

On the contrary, they were questioned; in fact, the church atmosphere was filled with quarrels and conflicts, as attested by James 4:1. Therefore, why were they allowed to continue in their leadership positions? When James described the next method of

---

[40] James 3:13–17.

the conspirators, "selfish ambition," that question is answered. In Greek writings outside the Bible, selfish ambition described a politician seeking an office through unfair means; unfortunately, this phrase described the teachers in the church. James confronted teachers who were screening members of the congregation to determine whether their allegiance was given to the teacher's agenda. For the leaders who valued the power of their position, they felt their position was worth protecting. They wanted to make sure they knew who was on their side; more importantly, they wanted to identify those who would be obstacles to their goal.

The indictment that secret deals were made and strong alliances forged cannot be overlooked. Any unfair means that served their purpose was greeted with open arms. Any objector to their agenda would have been treated with malicious contempt; thus, they held their leadership positions.

Speaking of the motives of the conspirators, James labeled them as arrogant, earthly, natural, and demonic. The phrase "do not be arrogant" conveys two major points. One was the emphatic command to stop a habitual activity, while another point is that the arrogance was done entirely for the pleasures and purposes of the teachers. At the time of the writing of James, the fragile and discouraged church was being torn apart, but that did not concern the teachers. If the church would have been torn apart, they would have found another group to manipulate, which is arrogance personified. Furthermore, James spoke plainly when he called their activity demonic. Since their strength did not come from God, the teachers had to assemble a mob for protection purposes by rationalizing that their strength was in numbers. The assembled mob edified the ego of the leader or, more accurately, described the ego of a manipulator.

How do the attributes of bitter jealousy, selfish ambition, and arrogance tie in to Joseph? Using the same Greek word James used, Stephen affirmed the tie when he said, "The patriarchs became jealous of Joseph and sold him into Egypt."[41] The premeditation, degradation, and manipulation epitomized by the brothers are the same elements of a conspiracy recorded in the book of James.

The premeditation of the brothers came to fruition when Jacob sent Joseph to check up on his brothers as they watched the flock. It is written, "When they saw him from a distance and before he came close to them, they plotted against him to put him to death."[42] The phrase "plotted against him" is rare in the Hebrew language, but it is emphatic. One aspect of this phrase is its association with deceit and evil, while another aspect underscores the decisiveness of their decision to kill Joseph. Their action was not an unthinking reaction; it was premeditated. For years, they endured the favoritism their father showed to Joseph. Coupled by the dreams that described them bowing down to him, they found the right opportunity to display their hearts. Hatred overflowed, and they determined to put an end to this prideful dreamer. Of one accord, they plotted against their father's favorite son.

Premeditative methods are hard to stop, as I will illustrate. I remember a day that started out so peacefully, but a phone call changed everything. A man of great reputation was coming to pay me a visit. This was not completely unexpected as hours, days, weeks, and even months of prayer had been poured out over the sad situation. Storm clouds of defiance rumbled through

---

41 Acts 7:9.

42 Genesis 37:18.

that man's head. He wanted to pursue selfish passion even at the expense of denouncing his faith.

My heart pounded at the sound of the doorbell, and a cold shiver crawled down my back. We exchanged casual pleasantries until the reason for the visit was revealed. He softly began to make a case for his right to live according to his desires. As I presented biblical teaching and passionate pleas to reconsider, his eyes filled with contempt for the truth. Then he proclaimed, "I did not come here for your permission. I'm going to fulfill my desires."

The stone cold expression on his face horrified me. I knew that our relationship was at risk, but truth had to be presented boldly and compassionately, just as Jesus instructed. Despite pleas offering help, he left my house to embark on what turned out to be a costly journey. Sometimes, people make up their minds to go down a treacherous path, no matter how passionate and loving the plea.

The tensions in Joseph's brothers escalated as he approached them. The brothers "stripped Joseph of his tunic, the varicolored tunic that was on him; and they took him and threw him into the pit."[43] This premeditated act was a catalyst for a violent rage. Their simmering anger from hearing the dreams and from years past filled with favoritism boiled out of control.

Consider what the brothers did after they threw Joseph into a pit: they sat down to eat a meal. No regret is mentioned, and no second thoughts are mentioned; they focused on their appetites! Years later, when the brothers were in Egypt pleading to Joseph, whom they did not recognize, "they said to one another, 'Truly we are guilty concerning our brother, because we saw the distress of his soul when he pleaded with us, yet we would not listen; therefore

---

43   Genesis 37:23–24a.

this distress has come upon us.'"[44] The complete picture of this event reveals the brothers continued to dine even when they heard the frantic and desperate cries from Joseph. Joseph could do no action or say no word to change their minds. The fear of knowing you are in the hands of wickedness without knowing the next step must have been horrifying.

Next, the brothers demonstrated degradation toward Joseph. Judah personified greed to the extreme when he suggested, "What profit is it for us to kill our brother and cover up his blood?"[45] Make no mistake to think that Judah had a heart change and denounced his hatred towards Joseph. Thoughts to free Joseph were not in Judah's mind; on the contrary, he thought of a plan that gave them a profit. Judah rationalized, "Come and let us sell him to the Ishmaelites and not lay our hands on him, for he is our brother, our own flesh."[46] Slavery is one of the worst, inhumane actions one human can inflict upon another. A person's freedom and even identity are forcibly altered. First, the lifespan of a slave was short; therefore, Joseph would die anyway. Second, they made money from selling Joseph into slavery, and he would be isolated in a foreign land. Nonetheless, Judah rationalized that selling Joseph would be better than killing him.

Joseph was sold to Midianite traders/Ishmaelites, two names describing one group of people. If these names ring a bell, there is a reason. God had promised to make of Abram a great nation while Abram was seventy-five and had no descendant. After ten

---

44   Genesis 42:21.

45   Genesis 37:26.

46   Genesis 37:27.

more years without a son, Abram's wife, Sarai, gave her Egyptian maid, Hagar, to be Abram's wife. She bore Abram a son named Ishmael, and Abram asked the Lord to make Ishmael the promised son whose descendants would occupy the Promised Land. The Lord rejected Abram's request, and when he was ninety-nine, his wife Sarai became pregnant with Isaac. He was the promised son whose descendants would compare to the number of grains of sand and occupy the Promised Land. Sarai saw Ishmael mocking Isaac, and she pleaded with Abram to have Hagar and Ishmael removed from their place. Hagar and Ishmael were sent away, and the descendants of Isaac and Ishmael have fought many battles over the possession of the Promised Land ever since. The hatred of the brothers toward Joseph was so intense that they willingly made a deal with the Ishmaelites.

Then, consider the measures taken in order to hide their guilt. When the brothers returned home without Joseph, they killed a male goat and dipped Joseph's multicolored tunic into the goat's blood. They made up a story that they had found the tunic but did not find the body of Joseph. They not only lied to their father, but they implied that it was Jacob's fault since he sent Joseph to find them. As with agents of conspiracy, they attempted to place the blame for their actions on another person. Undoubtedly, Jacob wrestled with the reasoning for sending Joseph on the journey alone to gather a report concerning the brothers and the flock. Jacob endured hard years of second-guessing and isolation from his beloved son because the brothers wanted to justify their sin by attempting to place their guilt on their father. Sin never destroys just the intended target but many others as well.

Years ago, I heard the following illustration about the

destructiveness of sin. A woman in the church became irate with a deacon. She decided to conjure up dirt on him, but she became frustrated when nothing damaging could be found. Instead, she simply spread a false rumor to a few friends to make the deacon's life a little uncomfortable. Weeks passed, when she received a phone call from a friend in another city. The rumor she intended to keep among a few had spread like wildfire and had more false details added to it. She wanted to inflict pain, not permanent damage, but it was too late. She humbly confessed to the deacon and his family her terrible act and wanted to know how she could fix the problem. The deacon grabbed an old pillow and asked if she would go to the backyard. He tore the pillow and threw the feathers into the blowing wind. He sadly remarked, "It would be easier for you to gather every feather from the pillow and put the pillow back together than for you to fix what you started."

Only the Father knows the extent of the damage caused by deceitful conspirators. Joseph was the victim of a premeditated plan filled with contempt. He had been trapped by those who had no regard for him as a person, much less a brother. While in the pit, Joseph was at the mercy of his brothers. Then, Joseph was at the mercy of the master he was bought to serve. Joseph knew the life of a slave was hard and short; yet, he was not in the position to change his circumstances. Joseph could see no good result even as he pleaded for his life, and this is the painful trial Joseph faced.

THE TRIAL OF COMPROMISE

"Jesus Christ is the same yesterday and today and forever."[47] This verse has been a personal favorite for many years. The certainty that

---

47 Hebrews 13:8.

God does not change has provided peace in the midst of difficulties. All the promises God made and all the provisions God has offered are trustworthy. In the context of Hebrews 13:8, believers were being encouraged to rely upon the truths that had been revealed to them from the Scriptures. They faced a challenge to accept an alteration to God's Word in order to accommodate false teachers in the church. They were exhorted, however, to be strengthened by the Word of God instead of chasing the alternative doctrine of their day. The writer reminded them that the Lord's instructions are not changed and cannot change. Tozer provided a reason to this point when he wrote,

> God cannot change for the better. Since He is perfectly holy, He has never been less holy than He is now and can never be holier than He is and has always been. Neither can God change for the worse. Any deterioration within the unspeakably holy nature of God is impossible. Indeed, I believe it impossible even to think of such a thing, for the moment we attempt to do so, the object about which we are thinking is no longer God but something else and someone less than He.[48]

The basis of the Lord's instructions is His nature; His instructions do not change because He does not change. Time does not change God's mind or His instructions.

Circumstances do not change God's instructions either. It is written,

> It came about after these events that his master's wife looked with desire at Joseph, and she said, "Lie with me." But he refused and said to his master's wife, "Behold, with me here, my

---

[48] A.W. Tozer, *The Knowledge of the Holy* (New York: HarperCollins, 1961), 49.

master does not concern himself with anything in the house, and he has put all that he owns in my charge. There is no one greater in this house than I, and he has withheld nothing from me except you, because you are his wife. How then could I do this great evil and sin against God?[49]

The background to this trial is important. Remember, Joseph was sold to the Ishmaelites; then, he was sold to Potiphar, who lived in Egypt. Joseph worked hard for Potiphar and earned his master's trust to the extent that Joseph became Potiphar's personal servant. Potiphar even made Joseph the "overseer over his house, and all that he owned he put in his charge."[50] Joseph caught the eye of Potiphar because of his work ethic and character. Unfortunately, Joseph caught the eye of Potiphar's wife because of her lust. Yet, when Joseph was faced with this trial, he knew the act of adultery would be disobedient against God, and that God would not justify his sin because Joseph was a slave. Neither could Joseph just quit being a slave, move to another city, or file a complaint. He had to deal with constant attacks from the temptation to compromise, and in dealing with this trial, I have limited this section to some areas in Joseph's life that were attacked by compromise.

One area where compromise attacked Joseph was concerning his character. Potiphar's wife did not merely ask Joseph to commit adultery with her, nor was she seeking his interest in having an affair. Motivated by lust, she exemplified a lack of concern for the thoughts Joseph had. Empowered by her position, she made a formal command to a slave and felt entitled to his instant obedience.

---

49 Genesis 39:7–9.

50 Genesis 39:4.

She expected blind obedience from Joseph even concerning her immoral demands. Revealing this mindset, MacArthur wrote, "Being a slave not only meant belonging to someone else; it also meant being always available to obey that person in every way. The slave's sole duty was to carry out the master's wishes, and the faithful slave was eager to do so without hesitation or complaint."[51] She owned Joseph; thus, she felt that he owed her his unwavering obedience. The issue was whether Joseph would serve the commands from God or the commands from Potiphar's wife.

Joseph had two masters, and the way each master wanted him to respond was diametrically different. The Bible says, "Now Joseph was handsome in form and appearance."[52] This intriguing statement may seem out of place or even contradictory to other verses in the Bible. Consider the time when God told Samuel, "Do not look at his appearance or at the height of his stature … for God sees not as man sees, for man looks at the outward appearance, but the Lord looks at the heart."[53] These two verses, however, crystallize a major difference between the perspectives of God and of Potiphar's wife. The eyes of the Lord go to the heart of a man, but the eyes of Potiphar's wife did not go that deep. God saw a young servant needing to be molded to prepare the servant for the work the Lord had planned for him. The woman saw a young, handsome servant who became the object of her sinful obsession. Yet, the two masters over Joseph also wanted the same thing from him: obedience. The pathway of obedience for each master went in opposite directions.

---

51 John MacArthur, *Slave: The Hidden Truth About Your Identity in Christ* (Nashville: Thomas Nelson, 2010), 46.

52 Genesis 39:6.

53 1 Samuel 16:7.

Ideally, it would have been better for Joseph if both masters wanted him to walk in integrity. Since that was not the case, Joseph was faced with a choice concerning his allegiance.

The life that God has called believers to live is contrary to the way the world operates. We have already written about God's desire to have a people who interact and rationalize with Him in order to represent Him. Thus, God has called His people to "Consecrate yourselves therefore, and be holy, for I am holy."[54] Believers have been called to set themselves aside to demonstrate a willing heart for God to work in and through their lives. Jesus correctly stated that man cannot serve two masters at the same time, especially when the two masters are different one from the other. Contrary to God, "For all that is in the world, the lust of the flesh and the lust of the eyes and the boastful pride of life, is not from the Father, but it is from the world."[55]

Joseph chose to ignore the request from Potiphar's wife.

Next, Joseph was attacked to compromise his desire. Joseph's time in slavery and imprisonment totaled thirteen years; how long did this wife continue to tempt Joseph? The Bible gives no answer to that question; rather, the Bible sheds light on another topic. According to Genesis 39:10, Potiphar's wife tempted Joseph "day after day." In the midst of faithfully fulfilling his daily service, he continued to refuse to engage in her sinful desires. Yet, Joseph had to wake up each morning with the awareness of her presence and possibly the reiteration of her sinful request. Joseph was the target of many sinful invitations; yet, one day Joseph's character was attacked even harder by the secrecy of the trial. Enraged by his

---

54 Leviticus 11:44.

55 1 John 2:16.

constant rejection, she found a day when they were alone, and this was when Joseph was tried the hardest. If he was putting on a show of righteousness for the master or fellow servants by neglecting her requests, this was when his heart would be revealed.

The text reads, "Now it happened one day that he went into the house to do his work, and none of the men of the household was there inside. She caught him by his garment."[56] Potiphar's wife had enough of the embarrassment of Joseph's refusals. Like a lion waiting for a deer to wander into an open field, she planned for and seized the moment when Joseph was the only servant in the house. The word "caught" in this text describes a violent act such as to capture, seize, or take possession. Her madness consumed her when she attacked Joseph. A fierce struggle ensued that resulted in the tearing off of the garment. The fact that Joseph ran out of his garment illustrated the quickness and viciousness of the ambush. It also demonstrated the convictions from Joseph's heart.

A conviction is the basis of an action denying compromise despite persistent advances or the desire to fit in with everyone else. Potiphar's wife learned of Joseph's convictions by his first refusal to engage in sinful activities despite her power. He showed great concern about the thoughts of God when he asked, "How then could I do this great evil and sin against God?" Furthermore, she learned the strength of his convictions when he denied her persistent invitations. Adding to her corrupt perversions, she played the race card by telling the other servants who heard her scream of how this Hebrew came to rape her. She expanded her accusations when she blamed Potiphar for elevating Joseph; thus, Joseph was sent to jail. In jail, Joseph's convictions were challenged and pruned once more.

---

56 Genesis 39:11–12a.

THE TRIAL OF COMPANIONSHIP

Reminiscent of the work ethic that caught Potiphar's attention, Joseph earned the respect of the chief jailer. It is written, "The chief jailer did not supervise anything under Joseph's charge because the Lord was with him; and whatever he did, the Lord made to prosper."[57]

Meanwhile, Pharaoh became infuriated with his chief cupbearer and his chief baker, and they were taken to the same location as Joseph. As Joseph made his routine rounds one day, he noticed the new prisoners were depressed. They were in confinement, for goodness' sake; did he expect them to be joyous? A major reason for their depression, though, was the inability to discern dreams that each had the previous night. Joseph compassionately asked them to share their dreams. It is written,

> In my dream, behold, there was a vine in front of me; and on the vine were three branches. And as it was budding, its blossoms came out, and its clusters produced ripe grapes. Now Pharaoh's cup was in my hand; so I took the grapes and squeezed them into Pharaoh's cup, and I put the cup into Pharaoh's hand." Then Joseph said to him, "This is the interpretation of it: the three branches are three days; within three more days Pharaoh will lift your head and restore you to your office ... according to your former custom when you were his cupbearer.[58]

After he heard the positive news concerning the cupbearer, the chief baker asked Joseph to interpret his dream. It is written,

---

57   Genesis 39:23.

58   Genesis 40:9–13.

When the chief baker saw that he had interpreted favorably, he said to Joseph, "I also saw in my dream, and behold, there were three baskets of white bread on my head; and in the top basket there were some of all sorts of baked food for Pharaoh, and the birds were eating them out of the basket on my head." Then Joseph answered and said, "This is the interpretation: the three baskets are three days; within three more days Pharaoh will lift up your head from you and will hang you on a tree, and the birds will eat your flesh off you."[59]

This time Joseph had bad news. Pharaoh executed the chief baker three days later.

The Lord brought the cupbearer to Joseph's place of confinement to give Joseph the opportunity to oversee the inmates. Since Joseph had demonstrated kindness by interpreting the dream, Joseph asked that the chief cupbearer return a gesture of kindness. Joseph asked the chief cupbearer to remember him before Pharaoh. Back in the good graces of Pharaoh, the cupbearer likely had many chances to bring up Joseph's name. Nonetheless, this is the description of the next two years, "He restored the chief cupbearer .... Yet the chief cupbearer did not remember Joseph, but forgot him."[60]

Farrar observed,

If you ever lived near the ocean, you know that waves come in sets. Surfers sit on their boards with their backs to the beach, looking over the horizon for the next set. Waves come in sets of as little as three and as many as twelve or more. Then it's calm for several minutes and the next set rolls in.

---

59   Genesis 40:16–19.

60   Genesis 40:21–23.

In Psalm 88:7, a lonely psalmist wrote, "You have afflicted me with all Your waves." If you read the context, he's talking about hardship, suffering, and loss. It's not unusual for God to send difficulties to us in sets—and it's worth noting that they often seem to come in sets of three.[61]

Trials are not always caused by malicious intent, but that does not take away the pain of the trial. Once the cupbearer was restored to his position, Joseph waited each day without much assurance that the promise would be kept, and he waited another two years for the next opportunity.

Joseph demonstrated an unbelievable resolve in His walk with God and an undeniable faithfulness to God. By the time the cupbearer was restored, Joseph had endured eleven years of agony. He used the awful conditions of slavery and imprisonment as tools that exhibited his character and his trust in the Lord by serving others. Whenever Joseph had displayed enough character for Potiphar and the chief jailer to trust him, he was dealt a setback as if there were a barrier that limited him to a life of agony. The strength of his resolve and faithfulness were necessary when the trials began to mount; there are those who become bitter through compounding trials.

No thought of bitterness entered the Floods' minds as their hearts blazed, the depth of their souls invigorated with possibility. David and Svea Flood took a grand leap of faith together. They were jointly commissioned with Joel and Bertha Erickson by their home church, Philadelphia Church in Stockholm, Sweden. "To win Africa for Christ" was their calling, and the seriousness of their

---

61   Steve Farrar, *God Built: Forged by God...in the Bad and Good of Life* (Colorado Springs, CO: David C. Cook, 2008), 43.

devotion was exemplified by their willingness to journey to remote villages with the gospel of Jesus Christ. The Belgian Congo was an extremely unforgiving climate to the Scandinavian couples because it was filled with wild beasts and insects they have never imagined existed.

They were delighted to discover a Swahili-speaking village. They journeyed to Africa just for this reason, to spread the gospel to people who knew of no such thing. They hoped that the grace, love, and blessings of God would be warmly received by the natives, but such was not the case. Instead, the chief of the first village they encountered scolded them for making the African gods angry, and their lives were threatened if they did not leave the village. In the next village they entered, N'dolera, the chief displayed worse treatment when he waved his arms frantically and shouted at the couples. The young Scandinavian couples were forced to take camp in the outlining mountain jungle. Over the next few agonizing months, all the villagers were forbidden from trading with the missionaries except for one boy. He could sell chickens and eggs twice a week for whatever he could get from the missionaries.

Rejection from the villages was not the only concern for the missionaries. David and Svea had a two-year-old son, David Jr. The dangers from the wild beasts coupled with multiple battles with malaria mounted upon the rejection they endured. Exhaustion, disease, and rejection stacked one upon another, fueling feelings of hopelessness for their efforts to win Africa for Christ. Joel Erickson lamented, "We're here to win Africa! … And we can't even win a single village."[62] David and Svea attempted to encourage their

---

62 Aggie Hurst and Doug Brendel, Aggie: *The Inspiring Story of a girl without a country* (Springfield, MO: Access Publishing, 1986), 18..

missionary partners, but to no avail. The Ericksons decided to go back to the main missionary base; the Floods were discouraged, but they had to stay. Svea was pregnant, and the toils from that journey would have been unbearable.

Since the chief only permitted one boy to trade with David and Svea twice a week, Svea took advantage of the opportunity to present the gospel to him. Before the departure of the Ericksons, the young boy accepted Jesus Christ to be his Lord. The boy would glow with joy when he talked with the missionaries, although he did not tell anyone in the village about his conversion. However, he did tell the village about the expectant child. Since the sight of a white baby was unique to them, curiosity filled the village. The chief allowed a midwife to help deliver the baby as long as village customs were followed.

At the time of delivery, Svea once again was stricken with malaria, and the midwife was extremely concerned about the health of the child. Svea gave birth to a girl, and the midwife took the umbilical cord outside the hut. The midwife dug a small hole in the ground, and when she spoke of Svea, she said, "She will always be one of us."[63]

Svea wanted to name the baby girl Aina Cecelia. Unfortunately, the physical strain of the pregnancy and the case of malaria took Svea's life seventeen days after Aina was born. Since it would have been impossible to carry the remains of Svea to Sweden, David dug a grave. Concerning his view of going to Africa, David Flood commented, "What a waste of life."[64]

Anger and bitterness became a raging fire inside David Flood.

---

[63] Ibid., 20.

[64] Ibid., 21.

"He had been faithful. He had willingly brought himself and his family into this backward world, ready to build God's kingdom by the sweat of his brow. And for what? Death and desertion and desperation—and the salvation of only one little African boy."[65] David hired help from the N'dolera village to accompany his family to the missionary base. Upon arrival, he gave his daughter to the Ericksons and with his son went home to Sweden. In Africa, he buried his wife and his service to God.

The Ericksons loved Aina until they died mysteriously eight months later. Aina was then given to Arthur and Anna Berg, an American missionary family. They changed Aina's name to Aggie and changed her home from Africa to South Dakota. Years later when she attended North Central Bible College in Minneapolis, she met Dewey Hurst, her future husband. Dewey and Aggie were married and had children, and Aggie's interest in her father reignited. They finally discovered that he lived in Sweden but had no way to go see him. Eventually, the Lord led them to a Scandinavian community outside of Seattle when Dewey became president of the Assemblies Northwest College. The Hursts celebrated their twenty-fifth anniversary together during their second year at the school. They were pleasantly surprised when the college gave them two tickets to Stockholm, Sweden, and they were going to see David Flood. On the day of their evening flight, Aggie noticed a religious magazine written in a foreign language. The picture on the magazine caught her attention because it was a white cross with the name Svea Flood! She rushed to the college to find someone to translate the article for her.

Meanwhile, David's health was horrible due to a stroke and

---

65   Ibid., 22.

diabetes. Even worse, David's anger and resentment toward God was such an unhealed wound that his family knew not to mention God's name around him. David relived the pain of witnessing his beloved wife die in Africa and the torment of giving away his daughter. When Aggie traveled to Sweden and entered his room, David's eyes filled with tears as he confessed that he never wanted to give her away. Pleasantly, she encouraged him, saying that God took care of her. "God forgot all of us," he spate. "Our lives have been like this because of Him."[66] David's mind went over the tragic story multiple times. He thought he knew the events all too well, but he did not know the events after he left Africa.

A journalist learned the rest of the story, and his article was translated to Aggie the day of her flight to Sweden. Aggie remembered the article and relayed it to her father. When Svea died and David fled Africa, there was only the conversion of one young boy. Thus, David thought their efforts had failed; even worse, he felt abandoned by God. On the contrary, that same young boy, who once was too afraid to tell the village about Christ, years later gained permission to build a school. He evangelized the students just as Svea Flood had shared the gospel with him. The children began evangelizing their parents, and before long, the whole village and even the chief of the village submitted their lives to Christ. The article reported six hundred conversions from the ministry of this school. When David heard the contents of the article, he began to confess his bitterness towards God and asked for His forgiveness. His heart began to soften even to the point of reflecting positively on memories concerning Africa.

Within a few weeks of Aggie's visit, David Flood went into

---

66   Ibid., 98.

eternity. A few years after David's death, the Hursts attended an evangelism conference in London, England. Aggie's interest piqued when she heard the testimony of a man representing the churches in Zaire, formerly known as the Belgian Congo. He shared stories of the impact of the ministries formed through the thirty-two mission stations, the hospital, and the one hundred ten thousand believers in the area. Aggie was amazed to hear the testimony about God's work in Zaire. She wondered if this man would know of the work of David and Svea Flood. As following testimonies were shared, Aggie squirmed in her seat from the desire to meet this man. When the service concluded, Aggie and Dewey raced to the platform to meet Ruhigita Ndagora. Aggie could not contain herself; she asked Ruhigita if he ever met David and Svea Flood. He replied, "Yes madam … It was Svea Flood who led me to Jesus Christ."[67] Perplexed, he asked how she knew David and Svea. When Aggie revealed that she was their daughter, he wept and joyously embraced Aggie. He asked Aggie to accept an invitation to come to Africa.

    Later, Aggie went to Zaire and viewed the place where her mother was buried. The villagers, who welcomed her with hugs and kisses, backed away to respect Aggie's time at the burial site. Their welcoming was not only extended to Aggie but to God as well. There was a church in the village, and the villagers viewed Svea Flood as a famous and fondly remembered woman. The one convert that David remembered was used by God to reach a village. God had given them a new heart; thus, they grew fonder of the witness and sacrifice made by the missionaries. After Aggie spent time at Svea's grave, the pastor of the church in the village led a worship service. He read John 14:24. "I tell you the truth, unless a kernel of

---

67 Ibid., 115.

wheat falls to the ground and dies, it remains only a single seed. But if it dies, it produces many seeds." Then, he read from Psalm 126:5. "Those who sow in tears will reap with songs of joy."

Unfortunately, David Flood knew remorseful tears more than he knew songs of joy. He responded to a noble and humbling calling when he obediently followed God's path to lead his family into the Belgian Congo. Accompanied by excitement and zeal, the missionaries shared the trustworthy account of the greatest Man ever to walk on the face of the Earth. Nonetheless, the villages were hostile, and his fellow missionaries, the Ericksons, left the N'dolera village. Despite his enthusiastic heart and determined will, David was rejected and felt abandoned even by God. David could not see the fruit that God, over time, would produce through his trial; therefore, he went home. He went home with a cumbersome and compiled pain. He had no inkling how or when God would use the faithfulness of two young couples wanting "To win Africa for Christ." God knew the plan and worked even the great hardships of the Floods and Ericksons in such a way that glorified Him and encouraged others to be faithful to Him.

No words adequately describe the depth of pain and sorrow experienced by some believers. No words adequately describe God's commitment to walk with His people through the midst of their hardships. Although the tendency may be to blame God or to neglect to walk the path He has called you to walk, fix your eyes and heart on God. Know that one day the trial will end, but the knowledge and peace that God gives in the midst of the trial will last. Seek God with passion and yield to Him the path you must take to get to His destination. Remember that He envisioned that His people would have an intimate relationship with Him, be able to reason with His knowledge, and represent Him to the smallest detail. He has endured so much for His people to enjoy that fellowship; there is no way He will forsake you or lead you in the wrong direction. Walk with God in the midst of the trial and be encouraged by the words of Jim Elliott as remembered by his dear wife, Elizabeth. "The important thing is to receive this moment's experience with both hands. Don't waste it." "Wherever you are, be all there," Jim once wrote, "Live to the hilt every situation you believe to be the will of God."

Chapter 3

SEARCH ME, O GOD

"FOR I KNOW THE PLANS that I have for you," declares the Lord, "plans for welfare and not for calamity to give you a future and a hope."[68] Spoken through Jeremiah the prophet, God reminded Israel of His goodness and faithfulness. Prior to this blessed verse, Jeremiah proclaimed scolding messages from God. Israel defied the covenant and commands given by God; instead, they chose to worship deities familiar to the pagan cultures surrounding them. Throughout the Scriptures, pride boiled in Israel's heart because of the unique covenants God made to Abraham and David. God assured those men that Israel would have a kingdom of peace ruled by the Messiah in the Promised Land. He warned the people that the Lord would not tolerate their disobedience, but Israel underestimated the seriousness of the warnings.

Israel's cockiness polluted their minds; thus, Jeremiah pleaded with them to repent of the wickedness that angered God. Others prophets, such as the prophet Habakkuk, proclaimed that God was even empowering the Babylonian kingdom and would use them to punish Israel. When King Nebuchadnezzar of Babylon

---

68   Jeremiah 29:11.

expanded his kingdom by conquering other kingdoms, false prophets successfully encouraged Israel to seek protection by establishing alliances with other countries. Strategically, they thought their best chance to resist the expansion of Babylon's kingdom involved allegiances with other countries. Jeremiah declared their hope would be futile; in the end, Babylon took Israel into exile.

By the time Jeremiah 29:11 filled the ears of Israel, they were in exile. Babylon demolished the land and heart of Israel; if there existed a time when someone could say "I told you so," Jeremiah had the opportunity. His previous messages warned the people of God's punishment for their sins; what would he say now that he was right and they were enslaved? The prophet presented a word from God that focused upon His goodness and faithfulness. Jeremiah proceeded with the encouraging words, "For behold, days are coming," declares the Lord, "when I will restore the fortunes of My people Israel and Judah." The Lord says, "I will also bring them back to the land that I gave to their forefathers and they shall possess it."[69] God did not forget His covenant; despite Israel's disobedience and His judgment against them, God refused to alienate His people. Because of His eternal mercy, God had something else in mind for Israel. On God's calendar, a date had been permanently marked for the day of restoration. Although God's people were in exile, they were not excommunicated.

Furthermore, God promised to keep a watchful eye on them and their oppressors.

Therefore all who devour you will be devoured; and all your

---

[69] Jeremiah 30:3.

adversaries, every one of them, will go into captivity; and those who plunder you will be for plunder, and all who prey upon you I will give for prey. For I will restore you to health and I will heal you of your wounds, declares the Lord, because they have called you an outcast, saying, It is Zion; no one cares for her.[70]

Due to Israel's suffering, Babylon rejoiced; joy filled their hearts while mockery and laughter filled their mouths. At last, Israel was defeated! The stories of old told how an enslaved Hebrew nation marched out of Egypt into the land they possessed. Leaders such as Moses and Joshua became distant memories, and kings such as David and Solomon remained people back in the good ole days. Israel was different; they acted and worshipped just like any other people in that day. From a Babylonian perspective, the stories describing God's protective power over Israel displayed no evidence when they demolished Israel. Babylon enjoyed the pinnacle of military power; unknown to them, God paid close attention to them and the way they treated His people.

Babylon thought they destroyed Israel; however, God knew that He was purifying His people. It is written,

> Behold, days are coming," declares the Lord, "when I will make a new covenant with the house of Israel and with the house of Judah, not like the covenant which I made with their fathers in the day I took them by the hand to bring them out of the land of Egypt, My covenant which they broke, although I was a husband to them," declares the Lord. "But this is the covenant which I will make with the house of Israel after those

---

70 Jeremiah 30:16–17.

days," declares the Lord, "I will put My law within them and on their heart I will write it; and I will be their God, and they shall be My people."[71]

Can you imagine how this message affected the enslaved people? They heard the mocking and laughter from the Babylonians; insecurity coupled with uncertainty flooded the minds of many Israelites. Fear set in just at the thought that God might have abandoned them forever; yet, Jeremiah spoke a different message. He shared encouraging words that God had not forgotten them; in addition, God would complete a work whereby His people would never forget Him.

Not every trial is necessarily a punishment from God, but every trial can be used by God to reveal His glorious plan. Let us once again revisit the nature of God's plan for His people, which is to "Consecrate yourselves therefore, and be holy, for I am holy."[72] Up to this point, the emphasis has revolved around God's expectation for His people to reason with His knowledge and to represent His ways. He wants believers to display His character to the world even in the midst of trials such as the ones Joseph faced. No other person or circumstance can rob a believer of the opportunity to use his or her circumstances as a display for God's character. The strongest enemy to a believer's ability to display God's character is not found among family or friends; no, the strongest enemy resides within the believer. Regrettably, my testimony proves that point; thus, this chapter sheds light on what hinders God's character from being lived out and seen by others.

---

71 Jeremiah 31:31–33.

72 Leviticus 11:44.

BURDEN OF VULNERABILITY

If a picture is worth a thousand words, this picture has a story worth telling. A blond-haired, blue-eyed boy smiled for the camera; with hands folded properly, his face gleamed with joy and pride at wearing his favorite suit. The green three-piece suit with a matching tie would be worn on many Sundays; church members called him "Little Preacher." Sunday school was a great joy as well because the teacher made learning about Jesus fun.

The teacher helped us fill out the Sunday school envelopes. Checks would be placed on the envelope for good behaviors such as attending "big church," reading the Bible, studying the lesson, and giving. When checkmarks filled the boxes on the envelope, a sense of accomplishment filled the boy's heart; Sunday was great! Unfortunately, Sunday is only one day in the week.

Although minor in comparison with others, I was born with cerebral palsy, which affects my speech and my walking. Neighborhood friends, my family, and church members did not say much to me about cerebral palsy, nor did they treat me different from anyone else. I did not know much about my cerebral palsy or think much about it until I went to school. Classmates teased me because I was different. I could not imagine why they called me weird and asked why I ran funny. I knew that I was slow and uncoordinated, but I thought they were crazy until I went home so that I could use the mirror to see how I ran. They were correct. I have a little twist in my right leg that no other person I knew had. Then, I heard myself on a tape for the first time and could tell that there was more to my speech than an accent. These discoveries were mind-boggling and upsetting. I was different, but I did not want to be different;

blending in with my classmates would have been fine with me.

Every day was another reminder that I was not only different but also strange since the other kids did not walk and talk as I did. There were no more denials because my eyes and ears provided the evidence; as I progressed through the first, second, and third grades, the teasing increased. I sensed that if I played with the other kids, they would laugh at me or pretend that I was helpless. On the other hand, Mom and Dad loved me with passion and treated me just as any good parent would. Church members welcomed me with open arms despite my being a different kid. Yet, deep within the confines my heart, I wondered why the treatment was wonderful. Did they feel sorry for me just like some of the kids at school? Did my classmates have a good reason to laugh at me? Cerebral palsy caused the limp in my leg and a stutter from my tongue; therefore, I regarded cerebral palsy to be my biggest problem—it was to blame for all my hurts. I thought that if cerebral palsy did not exist, true happiness could be mine.

The teasing and isolation from classmates was hurtful, but there was the presence of something more harmful hidden in my heart. When I was able to understand sermons from the pastor, a deep troubling crept into my soul. "Wait a minute," cried my heart. "God formed you." It is written, "For You formed my inward parts; You wove me in my mother's womb."[73] I heard in church services that God is always in control because He has all authority. I was taught how Jesus healed the lame and caused the blind to see; however, there was no instant healing for me. Why should a finger of blame point to cerebral palsy? I concluded that the blame should be placed on God. Dislike, frustration, and confusion do not

---

73 Psalm 139:13.

adequately describe my emotions then. Disgust, bitterness, resentment and, unfortunately, even hatred are more honest descriptions. Rejection seemed to have established residence in my life, and it came because of something that I could not control. Encouraging words from well-intentioned friends fell upon deaf ears. Hearing that God has a plan or that one day I will look back and see God at work in my life were not things I wanted to hear. My soul longed for relief in that day, not for some day to come.

From outward appearances, people only saw the blond-haired, blue-eyed boy in a suit who took pride in checking all the boxes on the church envelope. Behind the smile portrayed by the picture, nobody knew the deep resentment in my heart that pointed to God. I felt robbed by God, and I wanted answers for the question that haunted me for many years: why me? I stand ashamed that these emotions depicted my true heart; the root of my problem was a fear to be honest and vulnerable with God. Thankfully, God's knowledge of man goes beyond outward appearances and sees the core of the inner man. The source of my bitterness toward God sprang from the well of a wicked heart; while attempting to be good, that wicked heart feasted upon constant failures.

I was rejected by my peers and feared that if my friends, church members, and God really knew me, they would reject me as well. Opening up your heart to another allows the opportunity for a deeper rejection and hurt. The protective mechanism of disallowing anyone, especially God, to have an intimate relationship with you results in more isolation. Even worse, man has no cure for a sinful heart.

There are those who claim that by changing one's environment, happiness will be found. In some situations, a change of scenery can be a blessing; yet, change to what goes on around you will not bring you closer to God's holiness. The only change that will draw you closer to Him and His ways lies with a change of your heart. Futility and frustration never ended and even got worse when I hoped for everything around me to change. By His grace, my greatest fear to be vulnerable before God by revealing all the bitterness and hatred towards Him vanished. At the age of nine, the Lord revealed to me that He alone gives people a new heart. I asked Him to change my heart; lovingly, He received me as His own.

BURDEN OF CONTROL

"Not fair! Not fair! This is not fair at all!" Learning to live with cerebral palsy, I had a bitter spirit cemented within my heart. I was the object of many jokes due to walking and talking differently than others. Other children were able to play baseball and football, but my doctors strongly discouraged any inclination of mine to play organized sports. In my heart, there was a passion to prove all those teasers wrong, but the opportunity was never granted. While my classmates were able to ride a two-wheeled bicycle, I was dependent upon training wheels until the age of nine. When they played sports throughout the school year, I was regulated to the stands or to the field as a ball boy—a manager, as it was called. I could manage the balls given to the referees and manage the water given to the players, but that was it. As a manager, I was on the field without really being on the field.

When I was in high school, I was a manager on the Ponchatoula High School football team. The guys were great to me, and they accepted me with open arms, even when I was a manager my freshman year in high school. They worked hard at making me feel important and treated me as part of the team—probably because I watched their jewelry during practice. I did not mind because it was great to have students talk to me in the hallways and invite me to eat lunch with them. I did my best to encourage them during the game and pep them up for the next game when we lost. At the end of my freshman year, the team surprised and honored me by giving me a letterman's jacket, which was usually reserved for juniors and seniors. That was a year when I truly felt accepted by peers, and I knew that I could be myself. When I served as manager during my freshman and sophomore years, I made long-lasting friendships.

When I was a senior, that team was special to me as well. Since the games were on Friday nights, the team would have a meal after school ended; then, we went to the field house. Before game preparation, we had a Fellowship of Christian Athletes meeting, and I was asked to speak at the meeting before our last home game in Ponchatoula. The attendance was overwhelming because most, if not all, of the team came to listen to my testimony. I spoke from the heart as I shared with fellow classmates struggles that the Lord led me through. I was encouraged by their attentiveness while I spoke and their encouragements after I finished the testimony. However, there is a regret that I have had since given that opportunity. I told the team that I would give up my strong arm (my left arm does not suffer the limitations that I have in my right arm) if I could participate in one play on the field. As that foolish statement sounded, unfortunately, football was more of a god than I wish to remember.

Since playing football was out of the question, the burning passion in my heart focused on coaching football. While in the seventh and eighth grades, various football games would be taped so that in spare time I could diagram every single play. I filled notebooks with football plays more than the notebooks I used for schoolwork. When I was able to be a manager for the high school team, my attention to how, and what the coaches taught the players probably matched the players' attention. The next year, our family joined Woodland Park Baptist Church. On the summer youth trip, I was asked to share my testimony with the group; as a result, I shared it with the whole church after we returned from the trip. Over the next twelve months, the Lord opened up other opportunities for me to share my testimony with local youth groups. The thought entered my mind that the Lord could continue using my testimony after I became a football coach.

During my junior year in high school, God called me to preach; defiantly and foolishly, I placed God on hold. I attempted to negotiate with God by offering the idea to Him that if He would enable me to be a successful football coach, I would preach in the off-season. The deal I offered God asked Him to fulfill my desires; then, I would fulfill His desires—as long as He did not interfere with my plans. I wanted God as a co-pilot, where both parties are equal and neither party infringes upon the other. How many times have you heard people declare great promises, saying they would give to God if only they had more money, sing to God if they had a golden voice, or serve God if they had more time? When the moment feels right, one would gladly serve God, and He would bless the person and his service. With that perspective, the church could feed the hungry, clothe the homeless, and testify Christ to the ends of the world if God poured out more blessings on His people. Thinking that God needs to add talent, money, or anything else to your life in order for you to serve Him better undermines the gifts God has already given us. Having the mindset that God can be held hostage until He meets our demands also does not represent the true identity of God.

Woodland Park Baptist Church sent the youth group to Ridgecrest, North Carolina, just a few weeks after my junior year in high school ended. Relaxation in the beautiful mountains coupled with all the activities of a youth camp fueled our anticipation for that trip. Our youth minister approached me with a familiar smirk. As a football coach and a teacher, he had a look that said he wanted me to run through a defensive line. He placed his arm around me, smiled, and said that the camp leaders asked the youth ministers if they knew of anyone who would sing or give a testimony. Well, I cannot sing to save my life, so my testimony would have to do. He told me the time that camp leaders planned to hear any willing participants. I jumped at the opportunity, and the camp leaders gave me a time slot in the evening service in the middle of the week.

Walking back to the dorm room, I felt as if the mountains in North Carolina weighed heavily upon my shoulders. Crowds of up to a hundred people caused the "butterflies" to stir my stomach, but the number of people at the camp approached three thousand. The next forty-eight hours seemed as if it would never arrive. Because of my anxiety, quiet time with the Lord drastically increased. A prayer garden offered peaceful moments alone with the Lord as I poured out my heart before Him. I could not think of anything that I could use to negotiate with Him; therefore, I asked that He would show great mercy by giving me the words to speak and to use me to glorify Him.

The day arrived! All the participants were asked to arrive an hour before the service started. With gathering my final thoughts and asking the Lord once again for strength, I walked to the worship service. Looking at the schedule for the service, I marked through every song and testimony slotted before me. The leader of the praise band introduced me, and I walked on stage. The lights were so bright that I could only see the first four rows, and sitting in those rows was my youth group. God's peace filled me as I began to share His work through my life. After I finished, the response from the crowd overwhelmed me as the Lord used me in a way that I never thought possible. Over the next few days, youth and adults alike encouraged me, while some youth ministers asked if I would lead the collective quiet time for their youth group. I knew from that moment my life was about to change, but I was unaware of how much it would and needed to change.

Two days after sharing my testimony with the entire camp, I was in the same prayer garden once again; the day was June 15, 1989. Still gleaming from the response of many encouraging people, the Holy Spirit confronted me concerning future plans. "When you gave your life to me for salvation, how much of your life did you give Me?" That questioned was burdensome when the hand of God examined my heart. Earlier that same day though, the camp Bible study examined Moses, claiming that he could not speak for God due to some type of speech problem; yet, God provided Aaron for him. I was barely seventeen, had trouble speaking plainly, and was not ready to preach. All the excuses that I provided to God the previous twelve months melted away because of the evidence from His work. In that prayer garden, I surrendered my life to proclaim His gospel. I yielded myself to Him by promising to preach any message, to any people, at any time, as long as He would speak through me.

The disguise of selfish religion tarnished my view of God; arrogantly and foolishly, I asked Him to be a god instead of God. In the end, you underestimate and neglect the time and gifts God has given you by wishing for something you do not have available to you at that moment when you could be serving the Lord. Graciously, He wooed my heart to demonstrate His great power to me and through me. The blessings from obedience far outweigh the burden of selfish control. When you offer everything to Him, He permits you to discover the depth of His strength.

BURDEN OF INSECURITY

At the tender age of seventeen, I submitted to the Lord by surrendering to His call for me to preach. Although cerebral palsy affected my speech, I believed that the Lord knew what He was doing when He called me. Being young, most invitations for me to preach centered on sharing my testimony to other youth groups. The Lord began opening up more opportunities, such as being asked to do a thirty-minute interview on the local cable station. I was even asked to write my testimony for the Sunday school quarterly that went to youth groups in various states. Unfortunately, arrogance influenced some sermons I preached. Foolishly, I used my cerebral palsy as a guilt trip for others to question their lack of commitment to God, and many young people gathered to the altar during my invitation. I thought that if I could regularly get a large group of people to the altar, then I would get more opportunities to preach—and in bigger churches. At one youth revival, half of the youth came down to the altar during the invitation.

It seemed as though the path to stardom had begun; I was proud of myself! I received pats on the back, and some of the youth directors at the revival offered to help spread the news about my preaching. People started to invite me to their churches so that I could talk to their youth; in fact, some of these churches were bigger. Finally, the future looked brighter than the past. The deep longing, seeking acceptance from peers, met satisfaction at least periodically. I felt almost ashamed even when everyone told me what a great message I preached. Despite all the accolades, I knew there was something terribly wrong when I preached; there was only a short-lived satisfaction and very little peace. The conclusion that tickled my ears said that the bad feelings came from Satan; thus, I should focus on all the good that is evident when people respond to the message.

A few years after I started preaching, I recognized a pastor visiting my home church, Woodland Park. I had spoken at the church where he pastored; from my only meeting with him, it was easy to tell that he had a warm and inviting personality. Within two years, Woodland Park called him to be on staff. I listened to him teach, and I was blown away by the depth of his teaching; he made the Bible come alive and taught things that I rarely heard. I got the brilliant idea that if I could combine his depth of teaching with my persuasive ability, then I would be a sure success. As our friendship intensified, it became evident he possessed a great peace although he'd had some tough ministry experiences. Brokenness and humility flowed from him where bitterness and hatred would have consumed other men. The quest began to identify the source of his strength and the resolve of his will.

I asked if he would be willing to listen to one of my sermons that I preached that year. I knew the sermon was not my best one, but it would give him the idea of how I preached. He certainly got the idea, all right! After I gave him a few weeks to have an opportunity to watch the tape, he asked if I would like to watch the tape with him so that he could comment on the sermon. We watched about five minutes of the sermon; then he fast-forwarded the tape to the invitation. Even though it felt like an eternity, he only spent the next forty-five minutes "helping" me to understand the true purpose and presentation of preaching. His invitation to me was quite simple. "Is this the path that you really want to walk?"

I found no need to deny the truth. I had become addicted to the standing ovations and the words of encouragement after sermons. Fear resided within me as I sought the Lord's guidance for a sermon, because some passages of Scripture are harder to preach than others. Anyone can get behind a pulpit to say what the congregation wants to hear, but a true servant of God proclaims what He wants to be said. Quoting C.H. Spurgeon, MacArthur recorded, "God chooses not milksops destitute of backbone, to wear his glory upon their faces. We have plenty of men made of sugar, nowadays, that melt into the stream of popular opinion; but these shall never ascend into the hill of the Lord, nor stand in his holy place, nor wear the tokens of his glory."[74] Within my heart, I wanted to "ascend into the hill of the Lord" to proclaim, "Thus says the Lord." Within the same heart, though, I wanted the encouraging words and pats on the back. At times, the mouthpiece of God will speak truth and hear encouraging words from the same sermon; nonetheless, God's challenge asked which one would I desire more?

I walked away from that meeting a different person. Through my mentor, Bro. Ray Pepple, the Lord instilled in me a conviction that changed more than my preaching; it changed my life. He cemented in my thick head the desire to pursue faithfulness to the whole truth of God instead of chasing the fruitfulness of my suave presentation. The Lord corrected my path, setting my feet on the

---

74 John MacArthur, *The Jesus You Can't Ignore* (Nashville: Thomas Nelson, 2008), 73.

one that led to peace and brought greater glory to Him. He conditioned me to evaluate every sermon by the standard of faithfulness to God's Word because when God is pleased with a sermon, He grants an unexplainable and undeniable peace to those faithful servants. Thankfully, the Lord gave Bro. Ray (I called him "Paul") a heart to disciple me, and he taught me how to be a true follower of Christ and to humbly embrace a servant's heart.

"Search me, O God, and know my heart; Try me and know my anxious thoughts; and see if there be any hurtful way in me, and lead me in the everlasting way."[75] With eloquence, the psalmist depicted the destination of the everlasting way that travels through the tough terrain of searching our hearts. A well-respected minister and good friend, Pastor Gary Hair, correctly said, "It seems as if the servant of God is tested before God fulfills His plan." During the testing period, anger, bitterness, doubt, and even hatred can be revealed; therefore, ask the Lord to change your heart. By His grace, temptations and trials do end. As attested by the psalmist, "And He called for a famine upon the land; He broke the whole staff of bread. He sent a man before them, Joseph, who was sold as a slave. They afflicted his feet with fetters, he himself was laid in irons; until the time that his word came to pass, the word of the Lord tested him."[76]

---

75   Psalm 139:23–24.

76   Psalm 105:16–19.

Chapter 4
IS THIS ON THE MAP?

"FOR I CONSIDER THAT THE sufferings of this present time are not worthy to be compared with the glory that is to be revealed to us. For the anxious longing of the creation waits eagerly for the revealing of the sons of God."[77] Those words send chills up and down my spine as my heart rejoices over the promise of spending eternity with God. Many believers have closed their eyes in death with the sweet anticipation of the glorious life God granted them. For one such believer, her battle with cancer had robbed her of physical strength and forced this vibrant saint to the confines of her bed. The last time we talked face to face, she asked me to pray for the lost and told me that she was at peace. She said, "God will heal me; whether it is on earth or when God calls me home, God will heal me!" She went home to be with the Lord not long after that conversation, but she was right; she is healed. Her testimony motivates me to yield every day to the Lord since I will stand before Him one day.

Paul referred to creation being subject to the slavery of corruption caused by sin and said that all the attributes, power, and divine nature have been clearly seen through creation. Yet, he confirmed,

---

77   Romans 8:18–19.

"How then will they call on Him in whom they have not believed? How will they believe in Him whom they have not heard? And how will they hear without a preacher? How will they preach unless they are sent? Just as it is written, How beautiful are the feet of those who bring good news of good things."[78]

Isaiah responded with joy and awe for the opportunity to share God's message. Any other response would have been inappropriate. Unfortunately, Israel's response was revealed when Paul wrote, "However, they did not all heed the good news; for Isaiah says, 'Lord, who has believed our report?'"[79] The message that went to the core of Isaiah's heart was rejected, just as God told Isaiah it would be. Many witnesses identify with the pain of sharing the news of salvation only to be rejected. A Christ-centered message contains more power to transform individuals, homes, communities, nations, and even the world than any other message; how tragic the greatest message continues to receive rejection.

Earlier in the ministry, I responded to rejection by sharing a message that people wanted to hear and that would tug heavily at their hearts to make a decision. As stated in the previous chapter, that approach did not please God and it did not give me peace. Being faithful to the purity of God's Word instead of watering it down weighs upon the heart. After being in the ministry for over twenty years and befriending many ministers along the way, I still have times of loneliness and depression. Preaching the Word of God the way that pleases Him requires a strong heart and plenty of tissue. Anybody can speak behind a pulpit, but it requires much more to preach on behalf of God.

---

78   Romans 10:14–15.

79   Romans 10:16.

Good news exists for those desiring to represent God in a way that honors Him. It is written, "And without faith it is impossible to please Him, for he who comes to God must believe that He is and that He is a rewarder of those who seek Him."[80] Although the road had hardships, Paul left an encouraging testimony that those who place their trust in the Lord will be blessed. God grants eternal rest to His people, but God bestows blessings on His people while they live on earth. Paul's testimony affirms that God does not send His people without empowering them to accomplish His will. In this chapter, we examine the heart of a man whose struggles were fierce but whose faith did not fail.

TRUSTING GOD GIVES GRACE

Outside the exercise of faith in God, every work not only is insufficient to be called good or righteous, but God labels that work as an abomination. As awful as it sounds, Isaiah confirmed, "For all of us have become like one who is unclean, and all our righteous deeds are like a filthy garment."[81] Apart from true faith producing works for the glory of God, the best works man has to offer God are despicable in His sight. Paul portrayed the desperation of man apart from the work of Christ when he wrote, "There is none righteous, not even one; there is none who understands, there is none who seeks for God; all have turned aside, together they have become useless; there is none who does good, there is not even one."[82]

A dreadful judgment has already been declared upon man. The

---

80   Hebrews 11:6.

81   Isaiah 64:6.

82   Romans 3:10–12.

reasoning behind God's indignation rests on the account of stolen glory. God blessed man with a mind to reason, abilities to maximize, and opportunities to use in order for the fulfillment of His desires. He expects man to be stewards of all those blessings to the end that man will worship Him. Unfortunately, every person has hurled insults and ridiculed the commands of God enough to deserve His wrath. God's name has been made into a casual curse word, and His standards of righteous living have been ignored because of either man's knowledge or man's will. Foolishly, some withhold worship from God by using the gifts and opportunities God has given them to glorify themselves—the creation—instead of the Creator. For this reason, "good works," which do not demonstrate genuine faith in Him, are judged as an abomination. Although vileness seethes from the heart of man toward God and the insubordination of man warrants judgment, God extends undeserved favor. Paul wrote, "For by grace you have been saved through faith; and that not of yourselves, it is the gift of God; not as a result of works, so that no one may boast."[83]

At the cross, God expressed His superlative love to undeserving sinners; at the same time, He poured out His wrath against sin upon the sinless Messiah, Jesus Christ. Just as the biblical description of grace baffles the minds of many unbelievers, some believers underestimate the fullness of God's grace. As much as God's gift was needed for salvation, grace must be supplied even more so to walk in a manner worthy of that salvation. Thankfully, the Lord "gives a greater grace. Therefore it says, God is opposed to the proud, but gives grace to the humble."[84] Consider the Apostle Paul when he

---

83   Ephesians 2:8–9.

84   James 4:6.

wrote, "Because of the surpassing greatness of the revelations, for this reason, to keep me from exalting myself, there was given me a thorn in the flesh, a messenger of Satan to torment me—to keep me from exalting myself!"[85] Yes, you read that correctly. The messenger of Satan, better known as a thorn in his flesh, was given to Paul. In an attempt to uncover the identity of the thorn, many theories provide merit for their opinions, while the most popular theory suggests the thorn in the flesh was Paul's eyesight. It is known that Paul endured imprisonments that did not provide the best environment for reading books and the parchments or for writing letters to fellow servants in the faith. The loss or even the damage to his eyesight would have prohibited Paul from doing as much as he desired.

The identity of the thorn of the flesh provides room for speculation, but the intensity of the thorn echoes throughout this passage. Fervently, Paul pleaded with God on three different occasions to remove the torment. Do not look down on Paul for imploring for the thorn's removal; otherwise, one underestimates the emotional battle that incurred. Whatever the identity of the thorn, Paul saw it as an obstacle that limited the service he desperately wanted to yield to God. His heart broke over the troubles in Corinth and over the abandonment of the faith by some in Galatia. He longed for churches he discipled in person or through the pen, and pleaded for their continuation in the faith. He wanted to be more active in their lives; from a human perspective, he could do so much more for God if this thorn was removed. His motivation behind the request describes the heart of a true servant wanting to find ways to honor his Master.

God could have removed the thorn, and Paul prayed for its

---

85   2 Corinthians 12:7.

removal; so, why did God not remove the thorn? "Because of the surpassing greatness of the revelations, for this reason, to keep me from exalting myself" identifies God's intention. Paul had just learned great depths of knowledge from God; once again, we can only speculate about the content of that information. Yet, Paul exhibited profound knowledge by tracing God's progressive revelation in the Old Testament, climaxing to the identity of the Messiah, Jesus Christ. The complexities balancing God's sovereignty and man's will followed by the rise, fall, and future salvation of Israel as detailed in the book of Romans still stirs conversations today. In response to the thorn, the natural tendency for the apostle would have been to parade how well he knew God, how much he had already suffered for God, and all the works God previously accomplished through him.

Although God revealed these truths to a knowledgeable servant, He wanted Paul to walk the pathway of humility and wanted to pour more grace upon him. Regarding the pathway of humility, all believers who want to know God intimately walk this journey. Paul admitted, "For I joyfully concur with the law of God in the inner man, but I see a different law in the members of my body, waging war against the law of my mind and making me a prisoner of the law of sin which is in my members."[86] As Paul's fellowship with God increased, his regret over and understanding of sin increased as well. He was appalled at his failures and even labeled himself the "chief of sinners." He wrestled with enjoying the temporary delights of sin but wanting to have those delights removed so that eternal and pure delights could fully occupy his heart. This familiar battle to the believer who desires God to reign supremely through

---

[86] Romans 7:22–23.

him or her unfortunately serves as an excuse to repress the will of God. "How can God use someone with a past like mine?" "When I overcome this sin, then I will feel better about serving the Lord!" "Add my name to the list of hypocrites if I serve the Lord." Excuses such as these imprison believers from service.

Paul realized his inability to uphold God's standard of holiness since his inner condition confirmed a desire to sin and since he had the thorn in the flesh. Elsewhere, Paul proclaimed, "Not that I have already obtained it or have already become perfect, but I press on so that I may lay hold of that for which also I was laid hold of by Christ Jesus."[87] He understood the tough road was necessary to travel, and there would be failures and regrets. These discouragements establish the reason why believers need to properly understand the relationship between trust and grace. Grace and trust invigorated Paul's service to the Lord when he knew that he was unworthy to know God, much less represent God. Why, then, did he proceed to press toward the goal to represent God's character? Simply, the Lord promised, "My grace is sufficient for you."[88] Paul's trust in God's faithfulness to fulfill His promise propelled him to pursue a greater understanding of God so that he could correctly tell others about the Mighty Fortress.

TRUSTING GOD GIVES STRENGTH

Those who claim to know God intimately without enduring internal or external hardships because of their faith in God either are deceiving you or are being deceived themselves. Paul affirmed, "Indeed, all who desire to live godly in Christ Jesus will be

---

87 Philippians 3:12.

88 2 Corinthians 12:9.

persecuted."[89] I advise believers to read *Foxe's Book of Martyrs* and *The New Foxe's Book of Martyrs*. If one doubts the hatred toward the gospel and the strength God gives to those persecuted believers to represent His character despite their circumstance, those two books supply plenty of examples. In 1977, two believers, Chiu-Chin-Hsui and Ho-Hsiu-Tzu, along with their pastor, were sentenced to death for their faith. The pastor was promised freedom on the condition that he kill the girls. Upon his acceptance of the condition, one of the girls said,

> Before being shot by you, we wish to thank you heartily for what you have meant to us. You baptized us, you taught us the way of eternal life, you gave us holy communion with the same hand in which you now have a gun. May God reward you for all that you have done for us. You also taught us that Christians are sometimes weak and commit terrible sins, but they can be forgiven again. When you regret what you are about to do to us, do not despair like Judas, but repent like Peter. God bless you, and remember that our last thought of you was not one of indignation against your failure. Everyone passes through hours of darkness. We die with gratitude.[90]

With that being said, they bowed their heads and closed their eyes, and the pastor shot them. Immediately, the Communist guards grabbed the pastor and placed him against the wall for his execution. His screams were heard, but no words of remorse or repentance were heard.

When Laura and I discovered God blessed us with a girl, I knew

---

89 2 Timothy 3:12.

90 Chadwick, *The New Foxe's Book of Martyrs*, 339-340.

that I wanted to name her Elizabeth in honor of Elizabeth Elliott. The testimony of Jim and Elizabeth Elliott inspires current believers to pursue God no matter the cost. Jim said, "He is no fool to gives up what he cannot keep to gain that which he cannot lose." Journeying to a foreign land, The Elliotts and four other missionary families set forth to spread the gospel. They targeted a village known for their violence—especially to outsiders—and feared by fellow tribes. The men decided to set up a station closer to the Auca Indians so that face-to-face encounters would be more possible. They established some connections with the tribe; the response from those tribal members gave the missionaries optimism. They radioed their wives with the news that they were praying to establish a relationship with the leaders of the Auca Indians. That was the last time anyone heard from Nate Saint, Ed McCully, Jim Elliot, Peter Fleming, or Roger Youderian; the five men were speared to death. Courageously, their widows continued the missionary work; eventually, the Auca Indians opened their arms to hear the gospel, and some of the Indians surrendered their lives to Christ.

How can two Chinese women give grace to their murderer? How can widows have the heart to witness to those who murdered their husbands? These stories demonstrate extraordinary strength, but Elizabeth Elliott offered a caution when she wrote,

> Jim's aim was to know God. His course, obedience—the only course that could lead to the fulfillment of his aim. His end was what some would call an extraordinary death, although in facing death he has quietly pointed out that many have died because of obedience to God. He and the other men with whom he died were hailed as heroes,

"martyrs." I do not approve. Nor would they have approved. Is the distinction between living for Christ and dying for Him, after all, so great? Is not the second the logical conclusion of the first? Furthermore, to live for God is to die, "daily," as the Apostle Paul put it. It is to lose everything that we may gain Christ. It is in thus laying down our lives that we find them.[91]

This gentle reminder provides wonderful insight. Persecution for one's faith in Christ should not render praise for that person but to the mighty God faithfully sustaining that person in the midst of persecution.

Paul continued, "My grace is sufficient for you, for power is perfected in weakness. Most gladly, therefore, I will rather boast about my weaknesses, so that the power of Christ may dwell in me. Therefore I am well content with weaknesses, with insults, with distresses, with persecutions, with difficulties, for Christ's sake; for when I am weak, then I am strong."[92] This passage summarizes the premise of this book. God calls people to know Him and to make Him known; the calling is to have a relationship with God, reason with God, and represent God as mentioned in this book. If you want to throw your hands up in the air as surrender by realizing you cannot accomplish God's expectations on your own, welcome to the first step. The enormous responsibility God bestows upon man should burden him to the point of complete surrender. As a result, we perceive ourselves as weak and completely dependent upon God. When a weak and dependent heart cries out to God for mercy and

---

91 Elizabeth Elliott, *Shadow of the Almighty* (San Francisco: HarperCollins, 1979), 9–10.

92 2 Corinthians 12:9–10.

grace to walk in His ways, God's limitless strength overflows that heart. The reason many believers have faced grave difficulties with confidence points to the fact that God strengthened that person.

Pay close attention how the word *content* is associated with the list of weaknesses, insults, distresses, persecutions, and difficulties. Paul believes that even though personal drama avalanched upon him, God granted him peace even when dealing with a thorn in the flesh. At times, I catch myself asking God to deliver me out of a situation in order to have peace, love, or any other Christ-like characteristic. The fleshly desires conclude that the presence of uncomfortable circumstances equals God needing to add or take away something in order to be at peace. From the sin in the Garden of Eden, the tempter has continued to ask whether or not God has withheld gifts that would bring greater joy and happiness in life. He fooled Adam and Eve with that same line of thought, and all of us have believed that same lie.

Graciously, God constantly supplies believers with gifts of grace, but God is the greatest gift given to believers. Let me illustrate the difference through the account of the death of Lazarus. Word was sent to Jesus that Lazarus was sick; yet, the Lord lingered for two more days before going to see him. Lazarus had been dead for four days when the Messiah approached Martha. Notice this exchange. It is written, "Martha then said to Jesus, 'Lord, if You had been here, my brother would not have died. Even now I know that whatever You ask of God, God will give You.' Jesus said to her, 'Your brother will rise again.' Martha said to Him, 'I know that he will rise again in the resurrection on the last day.'"[93]

To her credit, Martha recognized the power Jesus had came

---

93 John 11:21–24.

from the Father, and she affirmed their unique relationship. In addition, Martha believed in the resurrection and that Lazarus exemplified faith to that effect. Everything seems to be great.

John continued, "Jesus said to her, 'I am the resurrection and the life.'"[94] Jesus distinguished what Martha believed from what He taught her. Jesus not only brings life, He *is* life; not only is Christ responsible for the resurrection, He *is* the resurrection. Although what Martha said and what Jesus said look similar, a vast distinction separates the two in profound ways. When a request is made unto God for peace, He does not need to add, subtract, or change anything around you because God *is* the requested peace. Trust God to be your Deliverer and your Deliverance.

TRUSTING GOD GIVES HOPE

As if Paul had not endured enough trouble, He recalled,

> Five times I received from the Jews thirty-nine lashes. Three times I was beaten with rods, once I was stoned, three times I was shipwrecked, a night and a day I have spent in the deep. I have been on frequent journeys, in dangers from rivers, dangers from robbers, dangers from my countrymen, dangers from the Gentiles, dangers in the city, dangers in the wilderness, dangers on the sea, dangers among false brethren; I have been in labor and hardship, through many sleepless nights, in hunger and thirst, often without food, in cold and exposure. Apart from such external things, there is the daily pressure on me of concern for all the churches.[95]

---

94 John 11:25a.

95 2 Corinthians 11:24–27.

Nevertheless, there was a pain that he experienced in Asia that topped all else. Paul recalled, "For we do not want you to be unaware, brethren, of our affliction which came to us in Asia, that we were burdened excessively, beyond our strength, so that we despaired even of life; indeed, we had the sentence of death within ourselves."[96] The Corinthian church may have known about the troubles he faced in Asia, but he informed them of his brokenness in the midst of service. He felt poured out and had gone beyond his strength to continue the battle of serving God in a pagan culture. He did not want to see the dawn of a new morning because he despaired even of life itself. Like many prophets before him, Paul felt the sting of rejection and the repulsion that some people have against God.

The center of the painting has a pastor standing directly behind the pulpit with an open Bible in his left hand. His right hand is firmly grasping the pulpit, while his face portrays the intensity of a heart boldly presenting the message from God. To each side of the pastor, images of other messengers representing the Old and New Testament alike are seen as if they are surrounding the pastor, and behind the witnesses are angelic beings. Below this beautiful painting entitled "The Legacy," artist Ron DiCianni placed Hebrews 12:1 as undoubtedly the inspiration for his beautiful work. In one of the most picturesque scenes of the Bible, It is written, "Therefore, since we have so great a cloud of witnesses surrounding us, let us also lay aside every encumbrance and the sin which so easily entangles us and let us run with endurance the race that is set before us, fixing our eyes on Jesus, the author and perfecter of faith, who for the joy set before Him endured the cross, despising the shame,

---

96   2 Corinthians 1:8–9a.

and has sat down at the right hand of the throne of God."[97]

Climaxed by Jesus, the call to "run with endurance the race that is set before us" has been God's calling to His servants throughout the generations.

This passage follows one of my favorite chapters in the Bible, Hebrews 11, and is better known as the "Hall of Faith." Numerous testimonies from great believers such as Enoch, Noah, Abraham, and Moses are known by their faith. Volumes of books shed light on how God used these faithful servants in their day to encourage believers in our day. Yet, the nameless servants recorded in Hebrews 11 touch a sensitive spot in my heart. It is written, "And these died in faith, without receiving the promises, but having seen them and having welcomed them from a distance, and having confessed that they were strangers and exiles on the earth.... And all these, having gained approval through their faith, did not receive what was promised, because God had provided something better for us, so that apart from us they would not be made perfect."[98]

The testimonies of these faithful believers epitomize the essence of a servant's heart. They longed to see the fulfillment of God's promise; yet, God's providence led them down another path—the road of hope. The Greek word for hope is not regulated to wishful thinking; rather, there is certainty related to the word *hope*. It is the acceptance that one may not enjoy all the fruits of their labor upon this earth; nonetheless, the commitment to faithfulness remains strong, knowing that the believer's joy will come in the future.

Paul understood that "indeed, we had the sentence of death within ourselves so that we would not trust in ourselves, but in God

---

97 Hebrews 12:1–2.

98 Hebrews 11:13, 39–40.

who raises the dead; who delivered us from so great a peril of death, and will deliver us, He on whom we have set our hope."[99] Despite despairing of life itself, Paul knew that God would complete His purpose. What was the basis of that hope? Paul remembered, "Who delivered us from so great a peril of death, and will deliver us." In times of distress, fear escalates, and when that trial becomes the only one contemplated, panic can overcome the soul. Yet, Paul's confidence soared when he remembered previous situations in which God's faithfulness to support them helped them endure. He recalled the times that the Lord had been with him in many other difficulties; those times served as examples of an assurance that God would be with them. In an earlier writing, Paul encouraged the church at Philippi. While he was imprisoned, Paul told the church in Philippi, "For I am confident of this very thing, that He who began a good work in you will perfect it until the day of Christ Jesus."[100] We must remember the works and words of God in the midst of difficulty, even if that is a time when all your hope vanquishes; placing hope in God produces confidence and steadfastness.

    Another basis of hope flows from the testimonies of others. When Paul endured hardships such as beatings, stoning, and being left for dead, do you suppose part of his zeal to press on came from the example of another believer? Reading the account of Stephen, one might overlook this passage: "and the witnesses laid aside their robes at the feet of a young man named Saul."[101] This part seems to be extra information if you were reading Acts 7 for the first

---

99   2 Corinthians 1:9–10.

100 Philippians 1:6.

101 Acts 7:58.

time; however, God changed Saul's name to Paul and changed his character to reflect His Son, Jesus Christ. Paul became an articulate apologist, church planter, pastor, and disciple maker. Not much is said about Stephen after his death, but we can rest assured that Paul did not forget him.

The glow in his face and the forgiveness from his lips edged Stephen into the heart and mind of Paul. One might contest that since Stephen died painfully, that cannot build up hope in God. Their thinking places more weight on the persecution Stephen endured instead of the fruit God produced through Stephen. For Paul, everything centered on glorifying God; through an unjust murder, God's character was viewed on the account of Stephen's faithfulness. True hope, as Paul believed, propelled the believer to lift up the banner of Christ despite one's circumstances. When he came to the end of his strength and hope, Paul found a place of security that enabled him to demonstrate the life of Jesus Christ. He confirmed, "For our proud confidence is this: the testimony of our conscience, that in holiness and godly sincerity, not in fleshly wisdom but in the grace of God, we have conducted ourselves in the world, and especially toward you."[102] The joy that God grants His people by empowering them to represent Him cannot be quenched when trust is placed in Him even when our hope is gone. It is written, "Trust in the LORD with all your heart and do not lean on your own understanding. In all your ways acknowledge Him, and He will make your paths straight."[103]

Horatio G. Spafford (1828-1888) was a God-fearing man. In the 1860s, Horatio, his wife Anna, and their five children enjoyed

---

102 2 Corinthians 1:12.

103 Proverbs 3:5–6.

living outside of Chicago. As a caring and devoted family, the doors to their home were open to many people, such as Dwight L. Moody. The following decade was filled with great tragedies. Their four-year-old son died from scarlet fever. The Great Chicago Fire destroyed much of Horatio's real estate investments, although his home was spared. Despite the hit to their finances, they spent money to help the poor, homeless, and struggling neighbors. The 1870s did not begin well for them.

In 1873, the Spafford family planned a trip to Europe. He wanted to assist D.L. Moody at a revival in England. On the day of departure, Horatio had a business emergency that he had to handle. He did not want to disappoint his family, so he placed them on the Ville du Havre. Later, he received a telegram that read, "Saved alone." The steamer had been struck by a British ship, and it sank in twelve minutes. Their four daughters were among the 226 people who died. He rushed to set sail in order to bring his wife home. Horatio was called to the bridge of the ship by the captain when they sailed across the place where the ship sank. Returning to his cabin, Horatio penned the following words:

> When peace, like a river, attendeth my way,
> When sorrows like sea billows roll;
> Whatever my lot, Thou has taught me to say,
>
> It is well, it is well with my soul.
>
> Though Satan should buffet, though trials should come,
> Let this blest assurance control,
> That Christ has regarded my helpless estate,
> And hath shed His own blood for my soul.

My sin, oh, the bliss of this glorious thought!
My sin, not in part but the whole,
Is nailed to the cross, and I bear it no more,
Praise the Lord, praise the Lord, O my soul!

And Lord, haste the day when the faith shall be sight,
The clouds be rolled back as a scroll;
The trump shall resound, and the Lord shall descend,

Even so, it is well with my soul.[104]

---

[104] Baptist Hymnal, 410.

CHAPTER 5
ARE YOU THE POTTER OR THE CLAY?

THE STRENGTH AND ACCURACY NEEDED to speak on behalf of God comes from a submissive, God-centered prayer life. The need for servants of the Lord to render themselves as completely dependent upon God results from the awareness of whom they represent. My approach to prayer has been influenced and somewhat shaped by my mentor, Bro. Ray, Master Life studies, and reading works written by Henry Blackaby. One assignment in Master Life challenged me to pray for the worship service, which initially did not sound too bad. I could pray for everything in the worship service and everyone in the worship service within a few minutes; however, the request was to pray during the entire service. Were they crazy? For my first attempt, I must have prayed the same prayer sixty times during the hour-long service.

As my turn to pray for the services increased, a noticeable change in my prayer life developed. I learned to use prayer time as an opportunity to praise God and ask Him to change me. It mattered little that I prayed longer; on the contrary, it meant everything; I learned how to make God the center of my prayers. By the end of the Master Life study, I discovered that God changed me more than

I ever thought I could change Him. Prayers should be offered before God from a heart desiring to see the request through His eyes and for His glory. Vividly, I remember the vain sermons and empty words that used to come from my mouth, words that caused tears to flow to the congregation but came from a prideful heart. My past prayer life revolved around what I wanted; through God's grace, He revealed a better prayer life.

During the week, moments of silence fill the hallways of the church building. As part of my prayer time, I go from room to room, praying for the teacher and members of that class. Specifically, I pray for God to open their eyes to His truths and to write His statutes upon their hearts. When I go into the main sanctuary, I pass by every single pew to ask the Lord's favor upon those people that week, and that He will begin to plow their hearts to hear His Word. I journey to the altar to focus upon the awesome and enormous calling God has placed upon me. I pray until my heart is ready to hear from God; then, I am ready to study His Word in preparation for those messages.

With books spread all over my desk, the search for God's golden nuggets of knowledge and wisdom begins. I wrestle with the context of a particular passage of Scripture when God reveals ways that those verses need to change my life first. Hearing from the Lord will not always involve pleasant messages, but the word of the Lord will always be filled with purity and power. Such was the case when, as I sat in my office, a few people came to speak to me. They voiced their concerns about church issues as well as their thoughts about me. I listened to them suggest that the church calling me to that ministry was a huge mistake and that I needed to rethink the call to pastor. The memories of earlier opinions flooded my mind. I remembered when some people thought that, because of cerebral palsy, I was crazy to believe that God called me to preach. I recalled the time a church member accused me of being unaware that Satan was using me. I wanted to speak up in defense of myself; then, the powerful and pure presence of the Lord declared, "Be silent and be still!"

I wanted to blurt out a rebuttal and take control of the situation; as Lord, He wanted to take control of me during that accusation. I kept silent, and it would be nice to say that their ridiculous claims did not bother me. It would be a blessing to say that the contents of that meeting did not spread like a forest fire. Unfortunately, my spirit *was* hurt, and false, contradictory rumors multiplied from that meeting. My desire was just to blurt out the truth to put them in their place, but God wanted something more from me. His command to represent Him despite circumstances did not change when I was hurt. Instead of focusing upon my response, this chapter focuses upon two questions that God used to keep me on His path.

DOES A BELIEVER HAVE RIGHTS?

The Declaration of Independence announced innovative ideas that distinguished the colonies from England authoritatively and from the world politically:

We hold these truths to be self-evident, that all men are created equal, that they are endowed by their Creator with certain unalienable rights, that among these are life, liberty and the pursuit of happiness. That to secure these rights, governments are instituted among men, deriving their just powers from the consent of the governed. That whenever any form of government becomes destructive of these ends, it is the right of the people to alter or to abolish it and to institute new government, laying its foundation on such principles and organizing its powers in such form as to them shall seem most likely to affect their safety and happiness.

The Founding Fathers signed a document describing rights for citizens to voice their approval or objection to political policies. Within certain boundaries, they believed that citizens had the right to live in freedom without the government lording over them. Their view of government promoted individual freedoms unmatched by any other political ideology. Before 1776, the governing did not need the consent of the governed nor did kingdoms have three separate yet equal branches of government. Rulers of kingdoms quenched threats to their rule; they would not relinquish that much power as written in the Declaration of Independence. Where did these principles of government originate?

The Founding Fathers studied men such as a political philosopher from the 1750s, Charles de Montesquieu; a legal scholar from the 1760s, William Blackstone; a philosopher from the 1680s, John Locke. In fact, some of our Founding Fathers credited John Locke's work, *2 Treatises of Government*, to be a blueprint for the Declaration of Independence; in his work, Locke quoted the Bible more than 1,500 instances. History supports that it was preachers from the pulpit who had great influences on the Declaration of Independence. John Wise, a minister, wrote pamphlets in the early part of the 1700s that taught taxation without representation is tyranny, consent of the governed is a biblical government, and all men are created equal and endowed by certain rights. Do those principles sound familiar? Later in that century, revolutionary discussions fueled by the writings of men such as John Wise solidified the arguments for a government separate from English reign.

The Founding Fathers voiced the concerns of many others who believed their rights were being trampled. Their disgust, fueled by articles and pamphlets written in support of true democratic principles, escalated to a boiling point. The signatures upon the Declaration of Independence forged a new path for the colonies and burned a bridge between them and England. The fifty-three men who signed the Declaration of Independence knew that rights came from God and the danger they faced for announcing those rights. It is natural to be sensitive and even defensive about our rights. In fact, Benjamin Franklin summarized the risk of signing the document when he said, "Gentlemen, we must all hang together or most assuredly we shall all hang separately." Since they confirmed that they "are endowed by their Creator with certain unalienable rights," the Founding Fathers were not going to allow any king or kingdom to rob them of those rights.

The stands and sacrifices made by former generations to articulate, fight for, and defend the rights of American citizens must be remembered by and taught to current and future generations. Otherwise, the price and honor of freedom will be taken for granted and perhaps even forgotten. Similarly, believers must familiarize themselves with a biblical understanding of spiritual freedom. Since the Declaration of Independence came from biblical principles, what does God say about the rights of His children?

In this discussion about rights, I am associating them with the companionship of blessings, which is at the heart of this matter. Can a believer act according to selfishness, ask for God's forgiveness, and move on as if nothing ever happened? In the midst of trials and injustices, that question probes the mind of many believers. Callously, some want to act upon a sinful impulse, telling themselves that, in the end, God understands that believers are only human; therefore, they view their reactions as no big deal. In fact, some believers have, in a twisted sense of logic, claimed that because of their sin, God was able to show more grace to them. Concerning this theory, Paul questioned, "What shall we say then? Are we to continue in sin so that grace may increase?"[105]

Within this context, Paul balanced the connections between grace, sin, and the law. Philosophical struggles existed among believers in the first century concerning spiritual liberty and spiritual legalism. Some Jewish believers wanted to force Gentile believers to adhere to the Law of Moses and become Jews as a part of salvation. On the other hand, some believers claimed they were free from expectations to keep any portion of the law, thereby being free to live as they saw fit. Paul, however, embraced another perspective on the rights of a believer. While he rejected the need to make Gentile believers into Jews by attempting to observe the Law of Moses, he argued for the need to understand the restraints and responsibilities associated with freedom in Christ. He maintained that believers do not have the right to act according to their flesh even though God's grace has covered their sins. His rhetorical questions shined light on the preposterous assertion that God's grace only increases to match the depths of sin. God's grace, as presented in chapter 4 of this book, is showered upon believers in order for them to walk faithfully according to God's ways. The greatest blessing poured on a believer comes when personal rights are surrendered to God in order for Him to receive the greatest glory.

When Jesus walked on the earth, He had the right to be worshipped, to be loved by His own, and to enjoy the best riches of the

---

105   Romans 6:1.

world. Yet, the life of Jesus tells a different story. Being the Creator, Jesus should have had the best this world had to offer. Yet, when a scribe wanted to follow Jesus, He replied, "The foxes have holes and the birds of the air have nests, but the Son of Man has nowhere to lay His head."[106] Because He was able to perform miracles, people should have been so amazed by His authority that they listened to Him. Yet, while teaching in His hometown, Jesus proclaimed, "A prophet is not without honor except in his hometown and in his own household."[107] Being a loving Messiah, Jesus should have been received with open arms. Yet, He lamented, "Jerusalem, Jerusalem, who kills the prophets and stones those who are sent to her! How often I wanted to gather your children together, the way a hen gathers her chicks under her wings, and you were unwilling."[108]

Christ had no place to lay His head, was rejected even by His hometown, and volunteered to die for sins that He did not commit. Why was it that way? Paul wrote, "Have this attitude in yourselves which was also in Christ Jesus, who, although He existed in the form of God, did not regard equality with God a thing to be grasped, but emptied Himself, taking the form of a bond-servant, and being made in the likeness of men."[109] This thought packs a punch to think that Jesus "emptied Himself."

Some have claimed that Jesus emptied Himself of His deity or His equality with God. However, a closer examination of "He existed in the form of God" denounces that claim. The word *form* refers

---

106 Matthew 8:20.

107 Matthew 13:57.

108 Matthew 23:37.

109 Philippians 2:5–7.

to character; when Jesus physically walked this Earth, He healed the sick and raised the dead. Yet, the most venomous reactions from the Pharisees occurred when Jesus accepted true worship from people and forgave people of their sins. Furthermore, the word *existed* conveys the continuation of a previous condition and demonstrates that Jesus did nothing to earn His equality with God. Claiming the heresy that Jesus emptied His equality with God would have meant that He could not receive worship or forgive sins before suffering on the cross, since only God is to be worshipped and able to forgive sins. The Lamb of God had to be without blemish in order to be acceptable to God; thus, Jesus receiving worship and forgiving sins pleased God. Jesus did not go to the cross to become God; biblically, Jesus went to the cross because He is God!

Let there be no misunderstanding; this Son of Man, Jesus, was active in the creation of the heavens and the earth. When He said, "Let there be light," there was light. With the disciples at sea, Jesus commanded the storm to "Be still." What, then, does "emptied Himself" mean? MacArthur correctly noted that "Jesus Christ emptied Himself completely of every vestige of advantage and privilege, refusing to assert any divine right on His own behalf."[110] Everything Jesus did or said had a purpose, and His voluntary will to empty Himself is no exception. Although He used His divine powers to benefit others, Jesus identified with and wrapped Himself up in the limitations of man's flesh. The King of kings not only willfully walked and worked among His people but also came to serve them. Hours prior to His crucifixion, Jesus knelt before the disciples in order to wash their feet and manifested the masterpiece of His character that same night.

---

110 John MacArthur, *Philippians* (Chicago: Moody Publishers, 1984), 126.

The events in the Garden of Gethsemane prove that Jesus gave His life instead of merely being forced to die. When the betrayer, Judas Iscariot, kissed Jesus on the cheek, the crowd seized Jesus. Peter reacted violently by cutting off an ear of a slave of the high priest. Admonishing Peter, Jesus said, "Put your sword back into its place ... Or do you think that I cannot appeal to My Father, and He will at once put at My disposal more than twelve legions of angels? How then will the Scriptures be fulfilled, which say that it must happen this way?"[111] Peter could not see that every detail to God's plan was being carried out, but Jesus could. The crucifixion occurred because Jesus chose to empty Himself, not because of the schemes of man. The presence of the mob was part of Jesus fulfilling His mission. Peter saw chaos sweeping Jesus away, while Jesus knew that despite the fierce mob, God was in complete control.

Imagine the scene in heaven—twelve legions of angels waiting for Christ to command them to come! Jesus was their Master; their loyalty and love focused on Him. Apart from the fallen angels, angels exist to honor God. Whenever an angel appears to a person or a group of people, the angel always deflects praise in order to give praise to God. In some instances, angels have to tell people not to be afraid. The astonishment from an angel's presence is evidently breathtaking. They are powerful beings, as was evidenced by a single angel slaying 185,000 men in one night.[112] One Roman legion was 6,000 soldiers; thus, twelve legions equal 72,000 angels. The legions of angels could have annihilated the mob that seized Jesus. Undoubtedly, they would have gladly come to Jesus' call, but no call came from Him. In fact, Isaiah described this night thus:

---

111 Matthew 26:52–54.

112 2 Kings 19:35.

"He was oppressed and He was afflicted, yet He did not open His mouth; like a lamb that is led to slaughter, and like a sheep that is silent before its shearers, so He did not open His mouth."[113]

Jesus had the power to enforce His rights upon His tormentors. The scene in the Garden declares that the crucifixion took place because of Jesus' willingness to honor God by fulfilling His plan. The crucifixion did not happen due to a traitor, a mob, false accusations, or by the governing powers. Paul described Jesus' servant-heart when he wrote, "Being found in appearance as a man, He humbled Himself by becoming obedient to the point of death, even death on a cross."[114] For Jesus, silence while obeying God is far better than being in defiance to God's plan. Christ set forth an example of obedience.

"Why do I have to go through these difficulties?" "Is this how I should be treated?" "Why do I feel forsaken?" When being tempted or even in the midst of being persecuted for the name of Christ, believers cannot respond as they please and expect to be blessed by God. There is no "blanket of immunity" for sinful actions taken after becoming a follower of Christ. The believer's freedom and rights in Christ intertwines with the believer's responsibility to honor Christ. The freedom granted by the precious blood of the Savior provides the way for believers to glorify God in the midst of any circumstance. When trampled upon by ungodly people, the natural desire is to seek revenge or to act contrary to God's Word. Yet, the example of the Messiah and many other faithful servants of the King of kings bear another testimony. They serve as examples that faithfulness to the Lord glorifies the Lord and blesses

---

113 Isaiah 53:7.

114 Philippians 2:8.

the steadfast servant. Will we view our rights with an understanding that we are called to act in a manner that honors and testifies of the Lord?

DOES MY DESIRE IMITATE HIS DELIGHT?

When a discussion of one's rights transpires, do those conversations focus more upon the rights of the individual or upon the rights of God? God provided a visual answer for the prophet, Jeremiah, when the Lord told him to go to the potter's house. It is written, "But the vessel that he was making of clay was spoiled in the hand of the potter; so he remade it into another vessel, as it pleased the potter to make. Then the word of the Lord came to me saying, 'Can I not, O house of Israel, deal with you as this potter does?' declares the Lord."[115] The skillful potter understood what he was making and the beneficial purposes for that pottery. The clay responded to the boundaries set by the potter's hands, and when the clay did not respond in a manner that pleased the potter, he remade it into another vessel. The key components the Lord taught Jeremiah revolved around God's pleasure and God's prerogative.

Since God is the Creator of everything, He has the prerogative to expect worship from the creation that blesses His name. Throughout the Bible though, there are acts of service that God not only rejects but, quite frankly, He abhors. Abel offered an acceptable sacrifice to God, while God had no regard for Cain's offering. Nadab and Abihu offered a strange fire unto the Lord; thus, He enforced a quick and fierce judgment of death upon them. Similarly, Ananias and Sapphira received a judgment of death for lying to God and men concerning their offering.

---
115 Jeremiah 18:4–6.

When I was younger, I heard people say, "You cannot see the forest because of the trees." For years, that expression made absolutely no sense to me at all. I felt as ignorant as the disciples must have when they privately asked Jesus to explain a parable. Graciously, my parents explained the meaning behind not seeing the forest because of the trees. It described the problem of not seeing the whole picture.

Specifically, some know that God should be obeyed, but they miss the whole picture. God could demand service, but He desires that we want to serve; that type of service gives God pleasure. Obedience to God's plan brings glory to God as much as the heart of the servant desires to give that service. Consider when a widow gave two small copper coins, which amounted to a cent. Calling His disciples to Him, Jesus said to them, "Truly I say to you, this poor widow put in more than all the contributors of the treasury; for they all put in out of their surplus, but she, out of her poverty, put in all she owned, all she had to live on."[116] Graciously, the amount of the offering is viewed through the lens looking at the attitude of the giver; thus, what man may see as a small gift may in fact be viewed by God as an act of worship. David wrote encouraging words that tell us, "The sacrifices of God are a broken spirit; a broken and a contrite heart, O God, You will not despise."[117] Thus, the attitude of the heart determines the significance of the offering.

As for Paul, he was quickly rising in the Jewish establishment. Prestige and honor were within reach. Through his relentless pursuits and fierce persecutions against the church, Paul's name was notorious. According to Philippians 3, Paul took pride in his heritage.

---

116 Mark 12:43–44.

117 Psalm 51:17.

He placed great confidence in his work for God; from a human perspective, why not? He wrote, "If anyone else has a mind to put confidence in the flesh, I far more: circumcised the eighth day, of the nation of Israel, of the tribe of Benjamin, a Hebrew of Hebrews; as to the Law, a Pharisee; as to zeal, a persecutor of the church; as to the righteousness which is in the Law, found blameless."[118] He fulfilled and exceeded the customs of the Jewish faith. He traced his heritage and proved to be part of the prestigious tribe of Benjamin. He was trained by the famous and well-respected Rabbi Gamaliel. His zeal was testified by the commitment to become a Pharisee and a persecutor of the church. At one time, Paul viewed his status before God as something he earned and maintained.

On the road to Damascus, everything changed from his name to his nature, from his delights to his destination. He saw the error of his ways when he heard the voice of the Lord cry out, "Saul, Saul, why are you persecuting Me? ... I am Jesus whom you are persecuting, but get up and enter the city, and it will be told you what you must do."[119] Prior to this conversation, Saul desired to eradicate the church from existence because he viewed Jesus as a false teacher and followers of Christ as a threat to his religion. Nobody can question the sincerity or the commitment that Saul had to make sure his religious beliefs were unchallenged. He imprisoned believers and even sought them out by traveling to other cities in order to capture them. Although Saul's desire was strong, the problem was that God was not delighted with Saul's actions. If someone asked Saul before traveling to Damascus about his intentions, he would have claimed that he was doing it for God.

---

118 Philippians 3:4b–6.

119 Acts 9:4–6.

Paul was on the road to stardom as a Pharisee; God placed him on the road of purification as a servant. Considering the zeal and intellect of Saul, a vivid imagination is not required to think that Saul could have risen quickly in the Pharisee ranks. Yet, he traded the right to imprison people with whom he disagreed for the experience of being cast into prison by those who despised him. The Lord's journey for Paul had difficulties; did Paul regret following the Lord because of the distresses? He wrote, "But whatever things were gain to me, those things I have counted as loss for the sake of Christ."[120] From the confines of imprisonment, those words echo from the heart of a joyful servant not because of what he was enduring but because of the joy of the Lord. Paul continued,

> More than that, I count all things to be loss in view of the surpassing value of knowing Christ Jesus my Lord, for whom I have suffered the loss of all things, and count them but rubbish so that I may gain Christ, and may be found in Him, not having a righteousness of my own derived from the Law, but that which is through faith in Christ, the righteousness which comes from God on the basis of faith, that I may know Him and the power of His resurrection and the fellowship of His sufferings, being conformed to His death;[121]

Through salvation, Paul exchanged his righteousness for the righteousness of Christ. Man's personal righteousness is put to death so that Christ's righteousness will reign in the believer. In Galatians, Paul explained, "I have been crucified with Christ; and it is no longer I who live, but Christ lives in me; and the life which I now live

---

120 Philippians 3:7.

121 Philippians 3:8–10.

in the flesh I live by faith in the Son of God, who loved me and gave Himself up for me."[122] Paul began to have a new perspective. Paul exchanged prideful and self-centered religious activities to become like Christ. From Christ, Paul learned that death to self must occur in order to live unto God. Beyond the suffering, Paul viewed his circumstances as God molding him just as any skillful potter would make pottery. Christ taught a puzzling truth; death to self leads to life in Him.

Do not feel sorry for the apostle, because he did not dwell in a pity party. He saw the temporary hardships of this life as opportunities for God to do something greater. Jesus stated, "If anyone wishes to come after Me, he must deny himself, and take up his cross and follow Me. For whoever wishes to save his life will lose it; but whoever loses his life for My sake will find it. For what will it profit a man if he gains the whole world and forfeits his soul? Or what will a man give in exchange for his soul?"[123]

---

122 Galatians 2:20.

123 Matthew 16:24–26.

Chapter 6

STOP TODAY'S MESS FROM BECOMING TOMORROW'S MISTAKE

"Wherever you are, be all there! Live to the hilt every situation you believe to be the will of God." Spoken and exemplified by Jim Elliott, these words resonate as a passionate plea to joyfully embrace God's plan. Just as eagerness to dive into ministry accompanies many new believers, a spiritual utopia best describes the first few months of my life as a believer. At the age of nine, I wanted to broadcast the wonderful news of God's salvation to the entire world. Living to the hilt every situation you believe to be the will of God seemed to be the least of my concerns. A fire that burned deep within my heart fueled a passion to live for Christ and to forsake all the sins that entangled me.

Within a short period of time, discouragement whispered the message that sin still prevailed in my life. It seemed as if the daily devotions and time reading the Bible announced more sins that once went unnoticed. Doubt, fear, and anger saturated thoughts in my head, and I began to question what was wrong. Convictions bothered my soul more frequently. Ashamed of the sin within my heart, quiet times with God and reading His Word became scarce. The fire that once ignited a passion to tell everyone about the salvation God gave me had buckets of cold water dumped on it. Fearful of the drastic change, I sought advice to provide answers for the dwindling fire. The one answer that echoed the loudest in my head claimed that I had just settled down in my faith like many other believers.

For the next several years, a struggle ensued during moments of wanting to capture the spiritual utopia from those first few months after God changed my heart. On one hand, the desire to live to the hilt every situation in accordance with the will of God danced in my heart. I wanted to agree with David when he cried out, "Restore to me the joy of Your salvation and sustain me with a willing spirit."[124] On the other hand, the desire to be accepted and to hear affirmations tugged deeply on the inner man. As a result, attempts to reconcile these two longings eventually fizzled out. The most obvious conclusions that I saw was to be either a devoted, depressed believer or a casual, compromising hypocrite. With a depressed believer, the world crumbling down around them steals their joy, whereas the casual believer focuses upon enjoying life while neglecting a crumbling world that needs to hear about Christ.

The similarity connecting these conclusions led to more in-depth problems. Unresolved spiritual problems now will always result in worse problems in the future. Thankfully, God has an alternative for believers just settling in the depressed or casual status. The testimony of Joseph proves that a believer can have a passionate devotion to the Lord despite trials and still experience the pleasures that God grants. From studying the life of Joseph, principles emerge

---

124 Psalm 51:12.

that assist believers to live to the hilt every situation that they believe to be the will of God. The desire of proclaiming the gospel to every human being can intensify; however, another source of energy must fuel that conviction.

FAITHFUL ACCEPTANCE – ACCEPT GOD'S GIFTS BY BEING TEACHABLE

When his brothers sold him into slavery, Joseph could not have imagined the wild ride prepared for him. Joseph's special status in his father's heart only spurred forth hatred from his brothers. The insinuation from Joseph's dreams, that they would bow to him, bothered and insulted them. When they saw him approach them as they were tending to their father's flock, evil consumed their thoughts. They debated whether or not to kill him; ultimately, they attacked him, stripped him of his multicolored tunic, and threw him into a pit. Later, the brothers admitted to their awareness of the distress of Joseph's soul as he pleaded with them; yet, they would not listen. They decided to sell Joseph to Midianites, who sold him to Potiphar, the captain of Pharaoh's bodyguard. Once he was forced into a life of slavery, how could Joseph rise to the position that the dream from God promised?

Though Joseph was removed from the Promised Land, the Lord of the promise was not removed from him. God does not abandon believers in the midst of their trials, nor does He forget promises made to them.

After graduating from New Orleans Baptist Theological Seminary, the Lord led me to Memphis, TN. I furthered my seminary experience in Memphis and worked in a retail store to pay the bills. My heart and calling from God was set on being a pastor, and I preached whenever I had an opportunity. It had been nine years since accepting the call to preach, and I strived to live up to the promise to preach anywhere, to anyone, any words the Lord wanted to say through me. Many pastor friends encouraged me when resumes went out, but only a few churches replied. Discouragement set in and lingered as those opportunities were closed; then, God's gift came in the mail from a church in West Memphis, AR.

Calvary Baptist Church wanted to talk to me, but the church needed an associate pastor of youth and music. Regarding the music ministry, I sound like a cow dying in a hailstorm; as for the youth ministry, it had never crossed my mind. Graciously, they substituted being a minister of education instead of music; however, I was still concerned about whether I could effectively minister to youth. Once again, I reverted to selfish pride by telling the Lord the very specific ways that He could use me in the ministry. Many reasons could have been used to turn down the position, but the one reason that I accepted the call to be the associate pastor at Calvary Baptist Church came because the Lord led me there.

Over the next four years, the Lord taught me valuable lessons and surrounded me with many godly influences. The pastor at Calvary Baptist Church, Gary Hair, became a close confidant, not only in church matters but also with life struggles. He encouraged me to excel in faithfulness to the Lord and in His ways. I remember many times sitting in his office about to discuss the church calendar when he would share with me some insights that he discovered in his study. As he often asked for my thoughts, staff meetings tended to gravitate toward theological discussions; then, we would be ready to cover the details of our staff meeting. Reminding each other about the importance of faithfulness to God's standard helped us to identify our need for God's grace to do His will. We tested each possible church event to determine whether the event developed an accurate picture of God. The Lord used those times with Brother Gary to confirm many truths about ministry that are foundational convictions for me today and prepared me for the days ahead.

Joseph's dreams seemed out of reach. How could God use the horror of slavery in a foreign land to prepare Joseph for a time when his brothers would honor him? It is written, "The Lord was with Joseph, so he became a successful man."[125] Do not underestimate the value of the Lord's presence. Knowing the rest of the story—that Joseph was raised eventually to a high position in Egypt—should in no way dampen the impact of God's presence with Joseph during his years of slavery. God's presence reassured Joseph of the Lord's sovereignty and commitment to fulfill His plan; connected to that plan, "the Lord will not abandon His people, nor will He forsake His inheritance."[126] In Egypt, God demonstrated to Joseph that nothing could stop Him from being the Rock, the Fortress, and the Friend that Joseph needed in order to represent Him. The call to represent God in truth stands firm, regardless of the surroundings, and His presence provides strength to the believer who takes comfort in God's presence.

Joseph was taken to a foreign land by his slave owners, the Midianites; yet, God led Joseph into Egypt. The Lord had a purpose in mind that allowed these events to transpire, and He empowered Joseph during the trials. Let us once again revisit the nature of God's plan for His people: to have a relationship with Him, reason with His knowledge, and represent His ways to other people. Therefore, it is written that we are to "Consecrate yourselves therefore and be

---

125 Genesis 39:2a.

126 Psalm 94:14.

holy, for I am holy."[127] This standard intimidates those who rightly contemplate the holiness of God, especially since that standard must be maintained despite trials. Due to God's involvement in Joseph's life, Joseph received strength to respond faithfully. As God unfolded His plan, Joseph trusted the Lord; by embracing this challenge, Joseph developed into the servant that God desired by doing his best to serve Potiphar.

Consider the respect Joseph earned from Potiphar; it is written, "Now his master saw that the Lord was with him and how the Lord caused all that he did to prosper in his hand. So Joseph found favor in his sight and became his personal servant; and he made him overseer over his house, and all that he owned he put in his charge."[128] Joseph demonstrated a godly character despite his circumstances; thus, Potiphar placed more trust in Joseph. Potiphar had other servants, but Joseph was singled out from the others because he accepted the calling to live to the hilt every situation that is the will of God. Slavery was not his desire; nonetheless, he did respond by faith to God. Otherwise, he would have blamed God with bitterness and resentment instead of using that time to serve the Lord and Potiphar.

Joseph treated the trust his master bestowed on him as an honor. Wenham concluded, "Potiphar abandoned his interest in what Joseph was doing because he was so convinced that Joseph was doing the best for him."[129] After placing Joseph in charge of his home, the Lord blessed Potiphar's house, and He blessed the

---

127 Leviticus 11:44.

128 Genesis 39:3–4.

129 Gordon J. Wenham, *Genesis 16–50*, Word Biblical Commentary, vol. 2 (Nashville: Thomas Nelson, 2000), 374.

faithful servant. Similar to a roller coaster ride, Joseph endured the low points and was raised up by Potiphar's trust; next, he would come crashing down and sent into a few loops. Just as Joseph caught Potiphar's attention because of his character, Potiphar's wife noticed Joseph for other reasons.

FUTURE ANTICIPATION – HOPE IN THE LORD AND HONOR HIS JUDGMENT

Potiphar's wife wanted to have an affair with the young slave. Refusing to have an affair with her, Joseph focused upon his responsibilities to Potiphar. Her persistency increased; with each passing day, she invited Joseph to please her fantasies. One day, Potiphar's wife laid a trap to ensnare him. It is written, "Now it happened one day that he went into the house to do his work, and none of the men of the household was there inside. She caught him by his garment, saying, "Lie with me!" And he left his garment in her hand and fled, and went outside."[130] Needless to say, that garment was used to falsely accuse Joseph of initiating the confrontation. Potiphar's anger boiled as he believed that Joseph had attempted to rape his wife. He reacted by having Joseph confined with all the king's prisoners.

All the trust that Joseph earned by serving Potiphar and being used by God to bless his house did not spare him from jail. He was the victim but was sentenced as a criminal with no advocates to support his side; his confinement defined discrimination and injustice. Joseph must have been tempted to think that, in order to avoid jail, all he had to do was to have a one-night stand. Joseph never asked to be placed in a situation where he had to reject a woman's constant allurement, but he paid the price for his refusal. Every day

---

130 Genesis 39:11–12.

that he turned down that faithless wife's proposal was a day that he placed his life on the line. Since he was the slave, and since she threw herself at him, Joseph meant nothing to her except as the focus of her sinful pleasures.

Joseph attempted to explain his reasoning for rejecting her temptations. He argued, "Behold, with me here, my master does not concern himself with anything in the house, and he has put all that he owns in my charge. There is no one greater in this house than I, and he has withheld nothing from me except you, because you are his wife. How then could I do this great evil and sin against God?"[131] Joseph respected Potiphar's marriage and treasured his trust more than the wife demonstrated. The honor Potiphar bestowed, to withhold nothing from Joseph except his wife and not concern himself with the responsibilities delegated to Joseph, provided Joseph a reason to uphold his testimony. He worked so hard to earn that trust; why compromise it with one sin?

Good decisions involve thinking about the future consequences as well as the present day rewards. God warned, "Bread obtained by falsehood is sweet to a man, but afterward his mouth will be filled with gravel."[132] Sin entices, satisfies, justifies—and ultimately destroys. Then, reality reveals that the enticing promised treasures do not exist, and that the satisfaction was only temporary. Consider the event that polluted God's creation.

The root of the problem in the Garden is used as a familiar tactic against God, whose perfection and holiness filled creation. Adam and Eve were created in God's image and were entrusted with the responsibilities of stewardship over the earth and its inhabitants.

---

131 Genesis 39:8–9.

132 Proverbs 20:17.

They had the whole Garden to themselves to enjoy everything with God's blessing, except the fruit from one tree. Satan approached them with the temptation, saying, "For God knows that in the day you eat from it your eyes will be opened, and you will be like God, knowing good and evil."[133] Why did Adam and Eve rebel against God after He had blessed them with so much? Satan presented the theory that God withheld good to restrain them from being like Him because God was fearful of having an equal.

They sinned against God by eating from that tree, and the place of perfection became polluted by sin. Instantly, Adam and Eve knew what they had done was wrong. It is written, "Then the eyes of both of them were opened, and they knew that they were naked; and they sewed fig leaves together and made themselves loin coverings."[134] They hid from the Lord because they feared the consequences. When God confronted them about their sin, they pointed the finger of blame away from themselves; Eve blamed the serpent for deceiving her after Adam blamed her. Adam not only blamed Eve, but he ultimately blamed God. He said, "The woman whom You gave to be with me, she gave me from the tree, and I ate."[135] The startling part is Genesis 3 is the beginning of blaming others and blaming God for personal actions, but it did not end there.

Many people blame God as they are suffering from consequences resulting from their sin, while others blame God for the circumstance that led to their sin. That is why Adam blamed God

---

133 Genesis 3:5.

134 Genesis 3:7.

135 Genesis 3:12.

for the woman He gave Adam. The real blame falls squarely upon the individual for settling for a temporary pleasure that will always fail to produce that which was promised. For Joseph, he reasoned that the result of having even a one-night stand with Potiphar's wife was not worth tarnishing his testimony. He worked too long and hard to earn Potiphar's respect. But still, what if Joseph could have had the affair without anyone, especially Potiphar, finding out? From the perspective of secret sin, today's mess will not be tomorrow's mistake, or does it matter?

Notice once again Joseph's response to Potiphar's wife, "Behold, with me here, my master does not concern himself with anything in the house, and he has put all that he owns in my charge. There is no one greater in this house than I, and he has withheld nothing from me except you, because you are his wife. How then could I do this great evil and sin against God?"[136] In addition to avoiding the consequences of an affair, Joseph rejected her proposal because of God's judgment. Whether or not anyone, including Potiphar, found out about the sin, God would know, and Joseph knew he would have to give an account to God. It is written, "The fear of the Lord is the beginning of wisdom; a good understanding have all those who do His commandments; His praise endures forever."[137] A biblical understanding of fearing and loving God worked cohesively together for Joseph to refuse Potiphar's wife.

The anticipation of standing before a holy and righteous Judge should provide motivation to live according to His ways. Consider the following parable spoken by Jesus:

---

136   Genesis 39:8–9.

137   Psalm 111:10.

For it is just like a man about to go on a journey, who called his own slaves and entrusted his possessions to them. To one he gave five talents, to another, t w o , and to another, one, each according to his own ability; and he went on his journey. Immediately the one who had received the five talents went and traded with them, and gained five more talents. In the same manner the one who had received the two talents gained two more. But he who received the one talent went away, and dug a hole in the ground and hid his master's money. Now after a long time the master of those slaves came and settled accounts with them. The one who had received the five talents came up and brought five more talents, saying, "Master, you entrusted five talents to me. See, I have gained five more talents." His master said to him, "Well done, good and faithful slave. You were faithful with a few things, I will put you in charge of many things; enter into the joy of your master." Also the one who had received the two talents came up and said, "Master, you entrusted two talents to me. See, I have gained two more talents." His master said to him, "Well done, good and faithful slave. You were faithful with a few things, I will put you in charge of many things; enter into the joy of your master." And the one also who had received the one talent came up and said, "Master, I knew you to be a hard man, reaping where you did not sow and gathering where you scattered no seed. And I was afraid, and went away and hid your talent in the ground. See, you have what is yours." But his master answered and said to him,

"You wicked, lazy slave, you knew that I reap where I did not sow and gather where I scattered no seed. Then you ought to have put my money in the bank, and on my arrival I would have received my money back with interest. Therefore take away the talent from him, and give it to the one who has the ten talents. For to everyone who has, more shall be given, and he will have an abundance; but from the one who does not have, even what he does have shall be taken away. Throw out the worthless slave into the outer darkness; in that place there will be weeping and gnashing of teeth."[138]

The differences between the servants entrusted with five and two talents respectively greatly differed from the servant entrusted with one talent.

The core difference between the servants centers upon their view of the master. For the servant entrusted with one talent, he regarded the master as uncaring, dishonest, and weak. He accused the master of obtaining his riches as a result of stealing from others. Suggesting the master gained his riches unlawfully, the servant concluded that the master had no right to dictate what should be done with the talent. In addition, the servant claimed to be afraid of the master, which is the most baffling part of the parable. If the servant thought the master was intimidating, why ignore the expectation that the master had when he entrusted the talents to the servants? A servant afraid of his master would have gone overboard to please the angry and uncontrollable master; yet, that did not occur. He hid the talent and used the argument that he was afraid

---

[138] Matthew 25:14–30.

to hide the real reason for the inconsistency. The servant thought the master was weak.

The grand scheme was to ignore the commands of his master in order to participate in whatever activity he desired. He planned a speech casting blame on the master through proclaiming unfounded accusations, believing that the master would cower to him. In the Garden, Satan used the same justification to convince Adam and Eve to partake of the forbidden fruit. He suggested that God's motivation for prohibiting them from eating of that tree resulted from God's fear of them becoming like Him. The deceiver then questioned the severity of God's punishment: how can God allow the death of the center of creation and the ones He entrusted to rule over the earth and its inhabitants? The temptation was filled with arrogance, suggesting that God needed Adam and Eve too much and could never replace them, leaving God unable to fulfill His own judgment. Satan convinced them that God would understand why they ate the fruit and would repeal His punishment.

Their actions did not end well for them, and the punishment for the servant who received one talent turned out grim. Therefore, why do people attempt to push God by claiming they can do as they please because, in the end, God will understand? They embrace that mindset because they have a flawed view of God.

On the other hand, the servants entrusted with five and two talents, respectively, viewed the master properly. They placed value on the master's possessions because they placed value in the master. Trust must be earned before someone entrusts their possessions to you, but this was no ordinary lending status. The master's faith in these servants was to carry on his financial responsibilities while he was away on a long journey. These servants understood the magnitude of the situation meant their decisions affected other people. When the master returned from his journey, both of them began the conversation with, "See, I have gained ..." Boastfulness was not their motivation; rather, they wanted to show the master how deeply they loved him by attending to his financial matters as best they could.

The same master who was accused of being uncaring and dishonest by one servant was treasured by these two servants. Thus, they accepted the responsibilities to manage the talents, aware that they were accountable to him. When God's people embrace their circumstances in the same manner as the two servants embraced their responsibilities, a healthy balance of fearing and loving God coexist. As mentioned earlier, "The fear of the Lord is the beginning of wisdom." Therefore, a correct portrayal of fearing God results in walking in God's ways; in fact, without fearing the Lord, there is no start to walking in God's ways. Coupled with love of God, this relationship bears much fruit for the glory of God.

To some in the church, the previous verse is offensive, while to others it is confusing. Let me clear it up for you. Think back to a time when you were being tempted to sin. What reason popped into your mind to resist sin? If honesty prevails during this heart search, there are times that we refuse sin because we fear being caught or tarnishing our reputation. Thus, we are inclined to keep sin as private as possible, but God wants to help believers reach another motivation. God has granted us life, entrusted people with His creation, and dwells within the believer through His Holy Spirit in order to empower them to walk in His ways. Thus, the motivation should be the anticipation of the day when we stand before Him to say, "Master, you entrusted many opportunities to me; see, I have been faithful because You deserved to be glorified."

Unfortunately, everybody, including believers, sins. John emphasized, "If we say that we have no sin, we are deceiving ourselves and the truth is not in us … If we say that we have not sinned, we make Him a liar and His word is not in us."[139] Since the more God purifies a believer, the more that believer's awareness of sin increases, the idea of sinless perfection mocks biblical truth. The problem worsens when believers allow sin to go unconfessed, and that is how today's mess can be tomorrow's mistake. Lingering in the filth of sin dampens the heart and contaminates the mind; thus, view each moment as an opportunity to glorify God even when the past is filled with failures. We are not the first or only ones with regrets. Paul encouraged us by saying, "Therefore, since we have so great a cloud of witnesses surrounding us, let us also lay aside every encumbrance and the sin which so easily entangles us, and let us run with endurance the race that is set before us, fixing our eyes on Jesus, the author and perfecter of faith, who for the joy set before Him endured the cross, despising the shame, and has set down at the right hand of the throne of God."[140]

FULFILLED ANSWERS

Joseph stood firm in his convictions when Potiphar's wife tempted him to have an affair. In retaliation, she falsely accused him of attempted rape, and he was placed in jail! Joseph sat in jail as a victim with no lawyers rushing to his defense or mobs revolting in the streets calling for justice. A proven track record of dependability and integrity mattered little; he was just one of the prisoners. He

---

139 1 John 1:8, 10.

140 Hebrews 12:1–2.

was despised by his brothers and treated with contempt by Potiphar's wife; as Joseph found out, though, he was not abandoned, "But the Lord was with Joseph and extended kindness to him, and gave him favor in the sight of the chief jailer. The chief jailor committed to Joseph's charge all the prisoners who were in the jail; so that whatever was done there, he was responsible for it. The chief jailor did not supervise anything under Joseph's charge because the Lord was with him; and whatever he did, the Lord made to prosper."[141]

Once again, Joseph was in dire straits and could have blamed God and become consumed with bitterness. Yet, he used the time in jail to earn the respect of the chief jailor by demonstrating his knowledge of administration, and the Lord blessed Joseph for his faithfulness.

Joseph was entrusted with the great responsibility of leadership not only by Potiphar and the chief jailor but also from God. The ability to be a godly leader includes more than being a good administrator. Concerning the heart of godly leaders, Jesus instructed,

You know that those who are recognized as rulers of the Gentiles lord it over them; and their great men exercise authority over them. But it is not this way among you, but whoever wishes to become great among you shall be your servant; and whoever wishes to be first among you shall be slave of all. For even the Son of Man did not come to be served but to serve, and to give His life a ransom for many.[142]

A position of authority can be addictive and destructive when leaders rationalize that those who lead are greater than those who serve. However, the responsibility that God entrusts to leaders,

---

141 Genesis 39:21–23.

142 Mark 10: 42–45.

whether civil or church, should lead one to use that position to help people see God. Back when Joseph was given a prominent relationship and trust by his father, pride seeped into his heart. Telling the brothers that they would bow before him seemed to have pleased Joseph because he thought about the rewards of authority without considering the responsibilities of authority. Joseph was emotionally ready to be in charge. God knew better! He knew that Joseph needed to learn skills before receiving the enormous responsibility God had planned for him.

Then, two new prisoners are introduced in Genesis 39—Pharaoh's chief cupbearer and chief baker. It is written, "The captain of the bodyguard put Joseph in charge of them, and he took care of them; and they were in confinement for some time."[143] Notice the big change from a small phrase, "he took care of them." The Lord molded Joseph's heart through slavery and imprisonment and prepared him for God's plan. Readily, Joseph looked for opportunities to minister to the prisoners; thus, when he saw them dejected one day, he intervened in order to be a blessing to them. The cupbearer and the baker had different dreams that ended with different results. To the cupbearer, Joseph said his dream revealed that within three days, Pharaoh would restore him to his position. To the baker, Joseph told the truth; his dream revealed that within three days, Pharaoh would have the baker executed. Therefore, Joseph asked the cupbearer to remember him when he was restored to his position before Pharaoh.

"Yet the chief cupbearer did not remember Joseph, but forgot him."[144] God intervened on the behalf of Joseph by giving Pharaoh

---

143 Genesis 40:4.

144 Genesis 40:23.

a dream. Then, the chief cupbearer remembered Joseph and told Pharaoh that Joseph was accurate in his descriptions concerning the interpretation of a dream, even if it meant that Joseph had to share unpleasant news. In a hurry, Pharaoh called for Joseph to be brought out of the dungeon in order to given an interpretation to his dream; furthermore, it is written,

> Now let Pharaoh look for a man discerning and wise, and set him over the land of Egypt. Let Pharaoh take action to appoint overseers in charge of the land, and let him exact a fifth of the produce of the land of Egypt in the seven years of abundance. Then let them gather all the food of these good years that are coming, and store up the grain for food in the cities under Pharaoh's authority, and let them guard it. Let the food become as a reserve for the land for the seven years of famine which will occur in the land of Egypt, so that the land will not perish during the famine." Now the proposal seemed good to Pharaoh and to all his servants. Then Pharaoh said to his servants, "Can we find a man like this, in whom is a divine spirit?" So Pharaoh said to Joseph, "Since God has informed you of all this, there is no one so discerning and wise as you are. You shall be over my house, and according to your command all my people shall do homage; only in the throne I will be greater than you.[145]

Interpreting dreams gave Joseph an invitation to stand before Pharaoh. The gift to organize and mobilize people to accomplish a common goal gave Joseph the authority to be second to Pharaoh. Where did Joseph learn the skills to be in charge of this

---

145 Genesis 41:33–40.

task? He learned these skills during the years of slavery and false imprisonment.

At the age of seventeen, Joseph was enamored with the promise of power and prestige, which would have led him in the wrong direction. God loved Joseph and yearned for Joseph to represent Him properly. Therefore, one blessing that resulted from the trials was that Joseph was at a better place to be used of God and to glorify God, which is the greatest accomplishment a person can pursue. On the road of that journey, one will find that God will supply the strength, encouragement, and validation needed to reach the destination. Those who walk that path will have to endure hardship, but their lives today and throughout eternity will be much better because today's mess does not become tomorrow's mistake when one trusts in the Lord.

Chapter 7

LORD, I ONLY HAVE TWO CHEEKS

PLACE THE KEY INTO THE ignition, turn to start the car, and shift the gear stick to the proper place to drive; it sounds so simple. When all the parts work correctly, starting a car is easy; the difficulty is when those parts need to be repaired. At times, mechanics recognize the problem instantly; on other occasions, they must run tests to ascertain the problem. Forgiveness, also, sounds simple. You may have heard it said that an unforgiving heart hurts the offended one more than the offender. Jesus instructed, "For if you forgive others for their transgressions, your heavenly Father will also forgive you. But if you do not forgive others, then your Father will not forgive your transgressions."[146] Is the forgiveness that Jesus taught portrayed by the testimonies of believers and churches?

Although Jesus' warnings should be motivation enough to forgive others, there are many other reasons to forgive. Consider just a few of the bitter fruits of an unforgiving heart: envy, strife, jealousy, pride, greed, lack of love, lack of mercy, slander, gossip, outburst of anger, and the list can continue. These fruits would be replaced by characteristics such as love, purity, peace, patience, gentleness,

---

146 Matthew 6:14–15.

sound judgment, kindness, goodness, and joy, just to name a few. These lists combine the writings of Paul and James when they dealt with severe church issues. The fruits of those churches provided sufficient evidence of a deeper problem flourishing.

Forgiveness is a serious matter that greatly affects believers and non-believers alike, and there are many concerns over the identity and application of forgiveness. In chapters 7 and 8, we will wrestle with some tough questions in order to provide a greater understanding of forgiveness. In Joseph's case, he showered love on others, but showing forgiveness to his brothers presented difficulties that you might not have imagined.

WHEN SHOULD I FORGIVE?

Joseph confirmed, "'As for you, you meant evil against me, but God meant it for good in order to bring about this present result, to preserve many people alive. So therefore, do not be afraid; I will provide for you and your little ones.' So he comforted them and spoke kindly to them."[147] Personally, this token of love climaxes with Genesis chapters 37–50. Joseph verified the sincerity of his brothers and heard their brokenness over the way they had treated him. After testing them, Joseph revealed himself when his emotions would not settle down.

I believed for many years that it was at that moment when Joseph forgave his brothers. If such was the case, then Joseph did not forgive them in a manner that glorified the Lord; however, biblical evidence suggests that Joseph forgave his brothers before he ever had the opportunity to reveal his identity to them.

When did Joseph forgive his brothers? Forgiveness does not

---
147 Genesis 50:20–21.

begin with public recognition; rather, it blossoms within the heart. Inconspicuously, Joseph's heart was changed by the Lord. The exact moment cannot be pinpointed, but the evidence loudly announces God's work. Read a few verses stuck in the midst of the narrative's transition describing when Joseph was elevated by Pharaoh to be second in charge of Egypt and before the focus shifts to the need for the brothers to journey to Egypt. It is written, "Joseph named the firstborn Manasseh, 'For,' he said, 'God has made me forget all my trouble and all my father's household.' He named the second Ephraim, 'For,' he said, 'God has made me fruitful in the land of my affliction.'"[148] Manasseh's name describes the pain of forgiveness while Ephraim's name describes pleasures from God for forgiving. Joseph forgave the brothers before he saw them for the first time since he was seventeen; he initiated forgiveness before they knew his identity.

Understanding the awfulness of sin, sometimes called total depravity, and understanding grace combine to give clarity to the timing of forgiveness. As opposite as they seem, total depravity and grace are eternally interwoven to help describe one another. Whereas grace focuses upon God's gifts, total depravity describes the inability of man to merit the privilege of standing in the presence of God, much less maintaining a relationship with Him. Total depravity rules out any possibility for the merits of man to claim holiness. Paul painted a hopeless scenario when he wrote, "And you were dead in your trespasses and sins,"[149] which means to deviate from the path of God and to miss the mark of God's standards.

Paul went on to detail the evidences and effects of sin upon man

---

148 Genesis 41:51–52.

149 Ephesians 2:1.

when he addressed the power of sin. These trespasses and sins, Paul continued, "in which you formerly walked according to the course of this world, according to the prince of the power of the air, of the spirit that is now working in the sons of disobedience. Among them we too all formerly lived in the lusts of our flesh, indulging the desires of the flesh and of the mind."[150] Man's rebellion against God affects the mind and the flesh; in other words, sin is actions against God as well as man's reasoning for those actions. Apart from the will of God, every action and reasoning for that action is sin. Thus, one does not have to follow the world's pattern for living to actively participate in sin. One can walk "according to the course of this world" by defiance of God's standards. Furthermore, Paul described this lifestyle as walking "according to the prince of the power of the air," which is Satan. Although Satan does not "possess" every non-believer, he is actively orchestrating ways to influence people to defy God. He understands that the power of sin is too great for any human to conquer with only inner strength. Apart from Christ, people are powerless against Satan. Paul wanted to remind believers of the hopeless scenario from which Christ purchased and redeemed them.

Second, Paul addressed the price of sin by reminding believers that they "were by nature children of wrath, even as the rest."[151] Personally, a favorite word in the New Testament is rarely used: *propitiation* means to appease the wrath of someone. Although unpopular, the discussion of God's wrath should never be ignored or forgotten. Emphatically, Jesus said, "he who does not believe has been judged already, because he has not believed in the name

---

150 Ephesians 2:2–3b.

151 Ephesians 3c.

of the only begotten Son of God. This is the judgment, that the Light has come into the world, and men loved the darkness rather than the Light, for their deeds were evil."[152] In his famous sermon, *Sinners in the Hands of an Angry God,* Jonathan Edwards elaborated, "The wrath of God burns against them, their damnation does not slumber; the pit is prepared, the fire is made ready, the furnace is now hot, ready to receive them; the flames do now rage and glow. The glittering sword is whet, and held over them, and the pit hath opened its mouth under them."[153] Due to sin, the unconverted are the focus of God's fury, and this fury was poured out on the cross. God unleashed His wrath against the totality of man's sin as those sins were placed on Christ while He was on the cross. Since God did not spare Christ from wrath for sins placed upon Him, why would He cancel His wrath towards people who take pleasure in their sin? The price of sin is to receive God's wrath.

The sinner is hopeless. If God waited for man to walk righteously before extending grace and forgiveness to him, there would be no person who could be saved. Thankfully, it is written, "But God demonstrates His own love toward us, in that while we were yet sinners, Christ died for us."[154]

HOW SHOULD I FORGIVE?

Up until the fifth grade, some classmates enjoyed teasing me due to the affect cerebral palsy had on the way I walked and talked. Although I said, "Sticks and stones may break my bones, but words

---

152 John 3:18b–19.

153 Jonathan Edwards, *Sermons of Jonathan* Edwards (Peabody, MA: Hendrickson Publishers, 2005), 401–402.

154 Romans 5:8.

will never hurt me," their words cut deeper than any physical wound. They seemed to enjoy taunting me to the point of tears; as one would mock my walk, others laughed. Anger and resentment boiled within me, and I wished to cast down fire from heaven upon them; *then we will see who laughs the loudest*, I thought. I desired justification for that attitude; though sorry for me, my parents encouraged me to forgive them instead. I did not embrace their instruction because forgiveness was the last thing I wanted to give my tormentors; a fat lip was my pick. I asked my parents why I should forgive those classmates, and I will never forget their wonderful counsel. Forgiveness is based upon my character instead of their conduct.

Since that sound advice, the Bible gave me another reason to forgive,

> Then Peter came and said to Him, "Lord, how often shall my brother sin against me and I forgive him? Up to seven times?" Jesus said to him, "I do not say to you, up to seven times, but up to seventy times seven. For this reason the kingdom of heaven may be compared to a king who wished to settle accounts with his slaves. When he had begun to settle them, one who owed him ten thousand talents was brought to him. But since he did not have the means to repay, his lord commanded him to be sold, along with his wife and children and all that he had, and repayment to be made. So the slave fell to the ground and prostrated himself before him, saying, 'Have patience with me and I will repay you everything.' And the lord of that slave felt compassion and released him and forgave him the debt. But that slave went out and found one of

his fellow slaves who owed him a hundred denarii; and he seized him and began to choke him, saying, 'Pay back what you owe.' So his fellow slave fell to the ground and began to plead with him, saying, 'Have patience with me and I will repay you.' But he was unwilling and went and threw him in prison until he should pay back what was owed. So when his fellow slaves saw what had happened, they were deeply grieved and came and reported to their lord all that had happened. Then summoning him, his lord said to him, 'You wicked slave, I forgave you all that debt because you pleaded with me. Should you not also have had mercy on your fellow slave, in the same way that I had mercy on you?' And his lord, moved with anger, handed him over to the torturers until he should repay all that was owed him. My heavenly Father will also do the same to you, if each of you does not forgive his brother from your heart."[155]

The essence of this parable focuses upon the reason that believers must forgive, and it starts with the fact that God has forgiven them.

The king expected the servant to duplicate his forgiveness to others. When the forgiven servant refused to forgive his fellow servant, other servants brought the matter to the king's attention. They were appalled that someone who was treated with so much compassion would leave the king's presence and act another way. The unforgiving servant did not conduct himself in line with the standard exemplified by the king. Since the highest office in the land acted

---

[155] Matthew 18:21–35.

with compassion, the standard was set for the people to follow. For this reason, the Bible identifies righteousness or lack thereof with a king when his reign is introduced to the reader; the way the king's heart turned influenced the way the nation related to God.

Concerning God, the standard of forgiveness goes beyond our imagination. Peter's assertion to forgive seven times exceeded the law's expectation. MacArthur noted, "Using references in the book of Amos (see 1:3, 6, 9, 11, 13; cf. Job 33:29), the rabbis had taken a repeated statement by God against neighboring enemies of Israel and made it into a universal rule for limiting God's forgiveness and, by extension, also man's."[156] Peter must have used the ratio from the Sermon on the Mount, "Whoever forces you to go one mile, go with him two."[157] He should be commended for doubling the tradition's requirement of three times and adding one more time to exceed Jesus' teaching. Yet, Jesus responded seven times seventy, and the point has nothing to do with the number of miles they walked or times forgiveness was granted.

Jesus taught Peter that God's forgiveness extended well beyond his understanding of forgiveness, much less his ability to give it. When offended, the Spirit of God reminds me that there is nothing done against me worse than what I have done against God. Depending upon my response, that truth either keeps me on God's path or draws me back to His path. The one hundred denarii owed by one slave to the other was a tremendous amount of money, with estimations being around three months of salary. He deserved that his money be paid back to him; likewise, the sins others have committed against you cause pain. Jesus did not diminish how hard and

---

156 John MacArthur, *Matthew 16–23* (Chicago: Moody Publishers, 1988), 145.

157 Matthew 5:41.

deep forgiveness penetrates the heart; however, all those offenses against you cannot come close to the offense every single person is guilty of before God.

The sinner is hopeless to stand before the Lord, "But God, being rich in mercy, because of His great love with which He loved us, even when we were dead in our transgressions made us alive together with Christ (by grace you have been saved)."[158] The servant's debt to the king of 10,000 talents seemed unrealistically high for any person to have incurred. MacArthur puts this number into perspective. "From historical documents of the time it has been determined that the total annual revenue collected by the Roman government from Idumea, Judea, Samaria, and Galilee was about 900 talents. Based upon those figures, ten thousand talents amounted to more than eleven years of taxes from those four provinces."[159] As unimaginable as this financial debt would be for an individual, Jesus clarified the amount of one's spiritual debt to God, a debt that no ordinary human can pay; graciously, the Son of God fulfilled it. The king forgave even though he heard the plea from the servant that he would repay; the king knew better. Without grace, sinners are hopeless before God; any other view insults the sacrifice of Christ.

Whereas the price of sin was paid by Jesus' blood shed on the cross, true brokenness over sin is epitomized in Luke 7. Knowing Jesus was invited to dine at the house of a Pharisee named Simon, a woman anointed the feet of Jesus with her tears and with a costly perfume. Simon was appalled that Jesus allowed a woman with such a horrible reputation to touch Him. Certainly, the Messiah would never allow this event, Simon rationalized quietly. Knowing

---

158   Ephesians 2:4–5.

159   MacArthur, Matthew 16-23 Commentary, 148.

Simon's heart, Jesus shared the following parable:

> A moneylender had two debtors: one owed five hundred denarii, and the other fifty. When they were unable to repay, he graciously forgave them both. So which of them will love him more? Simon answered and said, "I suppose the one whom he forgave more." And He said to him, "You have judged correctly." Turning to the woman, He said to Simon, "Do you see this woman? I entered your house; you gave Me no water for My feet, but she has wet My feet with her tears and wiped them with her hair. You gave Me no kiss; but she, since the time I came in, has not ceased to kiss My feet. You did not anoint My head with oil, but she anointed My feet with perfume. For this reason I say to you, her sins, which are many, have been forgiven, for she loved much; but he who is forgiven little, loves little.[160]

In the parable, the moneylender assumed both debts, but when asked, Simon logically concluded the one owing the greater debt would have the most appreciation. Simon's problem was ignoring the vastness of his sin as he saw this repentant woman. The principle is that knowing the awfulness of one's sins enables that person to see that only the greatness of God's grace establishes forgiveness.

On the cross, Jesus cried, "Father, forgive them; for they do not know what they are doing."[161] He identifies with the sorrow resulting from people sinning against Him, but the Lord knows that forgiveness truly can only be given by His grace. There is a strong relationship between viewing personal sins and forgiving others of

---

160 Luke 7:41–48.

161 Luke 23:34.

their sins. How can one cling to an unforgiving heart and think that God is pleased?

DOES FORGIVENESS EXCUSE SIN?

Forgiveness is a battle—a spiritual battle. When sin is known, the polarizing temptations are either to suppress the sin or to lash out through injustice or revenge. Pay attention to the way Jesus handled this potentate situation. It is written,

> The scribes and the Pharisees brought a woman caught in adultery, and having set her in the center of the court, they said to Him, "Teacher, this woman has been caught in adultery, in the very act. Now in the Law Moses commanded us to stone such women; what then do You say?" They were saying this, testing Him, so that they might have grounds for accusing Him. But Jesus stooped down and with His finger wrote on the ground. But when they persisted in asking Him, He straightened up, and said to them, "He who is without sin among you, let him be the first to throw a stone at her." Again He stooped down and wrote on the ground. When they heard it, they began to go out one by one, beginning with the older ones, and He was left alone, and the woman, where she was, in the center of the court. Straightening up, Jesus said to her, "Woman, where are they? Did no one condemn you?" She said, "No one, Lord." And Jesus said, "I do not condemn you, either. Go. From now on sin no more."[162]

This event perfectly reveals the cohesiveness of God's justice

---

162 John 8:3–11.

and grace; working together, they portray the holiness of God.

Everyone involved in this passage knew the woman was guilty, and the penalty for adultery was stoning. The Law confirmed, "If there is a man who commits adultery with another man's wife, one who commits adultery with his friend's wife, the adulterer and the adulteress shall surely be put to death."[163] The woman made no attempt to combat their accusation; even after the accusers left, she stood before Jesus, awaiting His action towards her sin. She awaited His verdict, expecting the righteous Judge to announce a harsh punishment, but words of grace flowed from Him. His response still baffles minds today. Some think that Jesus gave grace only to the woman and justice only to the scribes and Pharisees. This misunderstanding needs clarification in order to see why forgiveness ushers in God's holiness and how forgiveness does not excuse sin.

Jesus gave the adulterous woman a great amount of grace. First, He provided a rebuttal to the scribes and Pharisees who caught her in an act that merited stoning. Imagine the horror experienced by this woman, aware that she had been caught in the act and would be granted no plea bargains. Next, Jesus referred to her as a woman in the midst of a public place where undoubtedly she had been called other names. While the name "woman" may seem odd, if not condescending, Jesus referred to His mother, Mary, the Samaritan woman, and Mary Magdalene affectionately with the same distinction, "woman." Finally, He refused to condemn her for the adultery she had committed.

Jesus forbad the scribes and Pharisees from stoning her in order to show God's grace and holiness to them. Oddly enough, the grace extended to the scribes and Pharisees serves as an amazing twist. The

---

163 Leviticus 20:10.

Pharisees hated Jesus. Despite showing signs to confirm His deity, this group of man-centered religious zealots attempted to thwart the Messiah's ministry. They chose to form a coalition designed to end His teaching and work among the people. In fact, they were not really concerned with the sin of adultery; otherwise, they would have brought the man along with the woman to be stoned. They wanted to lash out at Jesus and embarked upon a common tendency that overestimated their righteousness through the means of injustice. Attempting to find fault with Jesus, the scribes and Pharisees amassed evidence that condemned their cause. It would have been so easy to give them a pounding of the righteous indignation they deserved. Yet, the path that Jesus chose overflowed with grace for them by challenging their hearts, even though He certainly knew the wickedness contained therein.

Have you ever considered that those who persecute believers need God's grace? Motivated by God's grace, Jesus' corrective instruction acted with the intention of sparing the men from compounding their sins. Their form of justice was perverse since the man involved with the woman was nowhere to be found; perhaps he was one of the accusers or a friend of one of them. The Bible does not provide his identity; however, it is perfectly clear that the scribes and Pharisees used the man as an instrument for deception. The accusers attempted to trick Jesus into displaying selective justice. If Jesus freed the woman, they could accuse him of disregarding the law given to Moses. On the other hand, the allowance of this execution would have suggested partiality in His application of the Law since the man who committed adultery with the woman was absent. In either case, Jesus' commitment to honoring every detail of the Law would have been questioned.

The scribes and Pharisees emphasized parts of the Law that would serve their purpose. They were willing to bend the Law of God in order to trick the Son of God, and Jesus could have once again reminded them of their hypocrisy as a condemnation against them. From the Sermon on the Mount, Jesus said,

> Do not judge so that you will not be judged. For in the way you judge, you will be judged; and by your standard of measure, it will be measured to you. Why do you look at the speck that is in your brother's eye, but do not notice the log that is in your own eye? Or how can you say to your brother, "Let me take the speck out of your eye," and behold, the log is in your eye? You hypocrite, first take the log out of your own eye, and then you will see clearly to take the speck out of your brother's eye.[164]

This rebuke reveals the error of the Pharisees and scribes: they confronted others struggling with sin, yet disregarded their own sins. In order to justify their own hidden, personal sins, the Pharisees had to bring public attention to the sins of others. An unforgiving spirit mimics the same problem. Instead of questioning the reason one refuses to forgive another despite the forgiveness God has granted to them, they have to continue their bitterness by judging selectively. The Messiah's caution is not about sinless perfection; rather, it centers upon the accuser's heart to ascertain whether holiness is truly desired.

Seeing the wicked making perverse decisions does not give pleasure to God; instead, His heart grieves. The personal sin of the scribes and Pharisees blinded them to God and His ways. They

---

164 Matthew 7:1–5.

rejected Jesus' exhortation of an internal inspection before taking the speck out of a brother's eye. Confidence oozed from their sin-stained hearts when they spoke about their righteousness, even though Christ offered the perspective that they were blinded spiritually. For this reason, we should pray for our enemies.

Remember the response of James and John, two disciples, who were upset because Samaria rejected Jesus? "'Lord, do You want us to command fire to come down from heaven and consume them?' But He turned and rebuked them, and said, 'You do not know what kind of spirit you are of; for the Son of Man did not come to destroy men's lives, but to save them.' And they went on to another village."[165]

In the midst of persecution for His name's sake, believers must pray for their enemies—not just about their enemies. Forgiveness is the key to the prayer life that allows believers to pray earnestly for the eyes of their enemies to be opened to God's truth. Freedom from bitterness unlocks the chains that limit a believer's prayer life from praying for his enemies in a way that honors God. Otherwise, pride can develop in the heart by rationalizing how much of a servant they are by suffering. A believer that is either not convicted with personal sins or concerned with the sins of others forfeits the opportunity to enhance holiness. Forgiveness enables one to pray freely by releasing the accuser to the Lord, while prayers plead for God to be merciful.

For those claiming that forgiving others releases them from punishment, consider the road to the cross for Jesus. Walking towards the site of the crucifixion, Jesus saw women mourning for Him; yet, He said,

---

165 Luke 9:54–56.

> Daughters of Jerusalem, stop weeping for Me, but weep for yourselves and for your children. For behold, the days are coming when they will say, "Blessed are the barren, and the wombs that never bore, and the breasts that never nursed. Then they will begin to say to the mountains, "fall on us," and to the hills, "cover us." For if they do these things when the tree is green, what will happen when it is dry?[166]

The women who mourned over the crucifixion had good reasons, just as Jesus had good reasons to be concerned for others. He knew a day has been set aside when the Lord will reveal every small detail of man's wickedness in order to bring about a righteous judgment. In this conversation, however, Jesus referred to a time of punishment other than the last judgment. On the cross, He cried, "Father, forgive them; for they do not know what they are doing."[167] They were blind to their sinfulness that produced false testimonies, justified the death of an innocent Man, and mocked His death. Nonetheless, Jesus demonstrated a gracious response just like the one He gave the accusers of the adulterous woman. They enjoyed their sin, but Jesus knew they needed grace, and their torment of Him did not prevent a prayer of grace to flow from His lips.

God wants us to forgive so that when His punishment is rendered, we will be innocent. Paul warned,

> Never pay back evil for evil to anyone. Respect what is right in the sight of all men. If possible, so far as it depends on you, be at peace with all men. Never take your own

---

166 Luke 23:28–31.

167 Luke 23:34.

revenge, beloved, but leave room for the wrath of God, for it is written, "Vengeance is Mine, I will repay," says the Lord. "But if your enemy is hungry, feed him, and if he is thirsty, give him a drink; for in so doing you will heap burning coals on his head." Do not be overcome by evil, but overcome evil with good.[168]

When the believer forgives, prayers of mercy can be rendered for those who oppress them, and thoughts of retaliation subside while acts of mercy can be given. Thus, persecution results in the transformation of one into someone imitating the character of Christ better, and that provides a solid justification to forgive.

Unfortunately, some have misunderstood His refusal to condemn the adulterous woman by suggesting that He went easy on her and diminished her sin. On the contrary, Jesus exhibited justice when He told her, "From now on sin no more." This part of Jesus' answer to the woman seems to receive less attention as compared to His previous statement to her or the rebuttal given to the Pharisees and scribes. Yet, the importance of this response signifies the seriousness of the sin and the indignation God has towards sin. This corrective statement served to emphasize a need for her lifestyle to change and to change quickly. She was guilty of defiling the marriage bed and acting corruptly against God's standard of holiness. Jesus did not take her sin lightly; on the contrary, He warned her that this event needed to be a wakeup call to observe God's commands. The idea that Jesus allowed the adulterous woman to get away with her sin contradicts truth because Jesus informed her about justice.

---

168 Romans 12:17–21.

We can be confident that God will punish sin, but He will do so with righteousness and purity. For Joseph, the Bible does not provide the moment he forgave his brothers, but through grace, the evidence of forgiveness was seen. What evidences demonstrate your forgiveness?

Chapter 8

I THINK I CAN... I KNOW HE WILL

I THINK I CAN, I think I can, I think I can." As a child, I made Mom read *The Little Engine That Could* many nights. Watty Piper's story began with a train attempting to pull boxcars full of toys to the other side of the mountain, but she needed help. I loved to hear how the bigger engines were too afraid to take on the task; yet, the little engine accepted the challenge. She strained to pull the heavy load, but her determination and resolve not to quit proved to be her greatest strength. She accomplished the task that the other engines could not do or would not attempt. The story ended with the little engine saying, "I thought I could, I thought I could, I thought I could." My parents preached hard work and encouraged perseverance, and I loved how this story provided the perfect happy ending. That utopia sounds simple and uplifting; however, is it reliable?

No truer test exists than the moment our responsibility to reason with God's knowledge and represent His character intersects with relating to other people. For Joseph, he persevered through the trials without bitterness towards God or even his brothers. He used his time as a slave and as a prisoner in jail to exhibit his unwillingness to quit. Because of Pharaoh's dreams, the chief cupbearer remembered Joseph, who was granted the opportunity to provide an interpretation to Pharaoh that his dreams predicted seven good years of great abundance to be followed by seven years of famine. Joseph impressed Pharaoh with the ability to provide an interpretation and a well-organized plan to prepare for the famine. Once again, the Lord was with Joseph, as attested when God called him from imprisonment, where he oversaw the fellow prisoners, to a position of authority second in the land of Egypt. Pharaoh confirmed, "Though I am Pharaoh, yet without your permission no one shall raise his hand or foot in all the land of Egypt."[169] With the exception of Pharaoh, he had power over the people of Egypt.

Meanwhile, the impact of the famine was being felt by Jacob and the rest of the family. In frustration, "Jacob saw that there was grain in Egypt, and Jacob said to his sons, 'Why are you staring at one another?' He said, 'Behold, I have heard that there is grain in Egypt; go down there and buy some for us from that place, so that we may live and not die.'"[170] When the brothers reached Egypt, they appeared before Joseph, but they did not recognize him, although he recognized them. It is written, "And Joseph's brothers came and bowed down to him with their faces to the ground. When Joseph saw his brothers he recognized them, but he disguised himself to them and spoke to them harshly."[171] Joseph's dream finally came true because they did bow down to him, and he could have revealed himself to them or sent them away. The brothers came for grain, but Joseph wanted fellowship.

---

169 Genesis 41:44.

170 Genesis 42:1–2.

171 Genesis 42:6b–7a.

The problem of divisiveness was between Joseph and his brothers, but the pain from divisiveness spread to others. Years of fellowship were lost; Joseph did not know whether his father and Benjamin were alive. Although Joseph's forgiveness is verified through the names of his sons, Manasseh and Ephraim, there remained another challenge: the desire for restoration. Forgiveness can be given without restoration, but restoration can't happen without forgiveness. The Lord protected Joseph by endowing him with great honor and responsibility; yet, the missing piece to the puzzle was his unfulfilled dreams. Unlike Genesis 37, Joseph learned that true power controls the inner man instead of being an authority over men. The second most powerful and sought after man in Egypt longed for peace that his position could not give, and it was to have peace alongside fellowship with his family, including his brothers. Would they desire fellowship with him? To answer that question, Joseph placed his brothers through three significant tests that were enforced to ascertain the possibility of restoration.

WHAT ARE THE CHALLENGES TO RESTORATION?

When the brothers approached Joseph, Joseph began speaking harshly to them and accusing them of being spies. Joseph insinuated that they had come to spy on the land of Egypt since Egypt had prepared for a famine that impoverished many countries. They responded, "Your servants are twelve brothers in all, the sons of one man in the land of Canaan; and behold, the youngest is with our father today, and one is no longer alive."[172] This admission provided grounds for the test, and Joseph placed all the brothers in confinement for three days. It is written,

---

172 Genesis 42:13.

Now Joseph said to them on the third day, "Do this and live, for I fear God: if you are honest men, let one of your brothers be confined in your prison; but as for the rest of you, go, carry grain for the famine of your households, and bring your youngest brother to me, so your words may be verified, and you will not die." And they did so. Then they said to one another, "Truly we are guilty concerning our brother, because we saw the distress of his soul when he pleaded with us, yet we would not listen; therefore this distress has come upon us." Reuben answered them, saying, "Did I not tell you, Do not sin against the boy; and you would not listen? Now comes the reckoning for his blood."[173]

For all those years, Joseph thought all the brothers were behind the scheme; in fact, he could have blamed Reuben as the one most responsible since he was the oldest.

Yet, Reuben had persuaded his brothers to refrain from killing Joseph and to cast Joseph into the pit. Wanting to check on Joseph's condition, Reuben was upset when he went to the pit and found that Joseph was gone—sold to slave traders. This revelation was new to Joseph; upon hearing Reuben's assertion, Joseph turned away from them and wept. Some hurts, especially older ones, have a tendency to spread farther and penetrate deeper than the painful event. Damaging memories build walls around the heart and tend to serve as a protective mechanism. Joseph found within his heart his desire for fellowship wrestled against his fear of being vulnerable. Forgiveness can be offered without being received, whereas biblical restoration involves all participants. Joseph initiated the process of restoration through the willingness to listen with an open mind and an open heart.

---

173 Genesis 42:18–23.

Joseph needed to know if the brothers wanted reconciliation, and the first test dealt with the brother's truthfulness. After their time in prison, Joseph bound Simeon in the sight of the brothers and proposed that they bring the youngest brother to him. Joseph wanted to see his younger sibling, but he was concerned about their treatment of him since they had despised Joseph. If the brothers resented Benjamin for being the son of Rachel just as they had Joseph, the confinement of Simeon would insure his safety on the journey. Before their journey back home, Joseph ordered that the brothers' sacks be secretly filled with money.

Questions exist as to Joseph's reasoning for secretly filling their bags with money. If this was part of the test, it would challenge their truthfulness. Returning home, the brothers shared the bad news that Benjamin had to go to Egypt to retrieve Simeon. Jacob was outraged more so that Benjamin had to go to Egypt than that Simeon was being held in prison. The thought of losing Benjamin, a favorite son since Joseph's departure, was more than he imagined. The situation deteriorated when the brothers found the money while unpacking. Instead of sending the brothers back immediately to reclaim Simeon, Jacob would not consent until the grain they had was almost gone. Reuben attempted to persuade Jacob to allow them to return to Egypt, but Jacob was reluctant to send Benjamin. Judah then persuaded Jacob that unless Benjamin went with them, they could not get grain from Egypt, and the whole family would starve. Therefore, Jacob sent Benjamin with the brothers to Egypt.

To the delight of Joseph, Benjamin journeyed with the brothers and reached their destination safe and sound. The second test focused upon how the brothers would treat Benjamin. From a critical perspective, the brothers assured Benjamin's safety in order to retrieve Simeon. When Joseph saw them, he sent the house stewards to prepare a meal for them. The brothers told the house steward about finding the money in their grain sacks, and the house steward responded, "Be at ease, do not be afraid. Your God and the God of your father has given you treasure in your sacks; I had your money."[174] This reception puzzled the brothers since they were treated harshly on the first journey, but kindness was extended to them upon their return. The brothers ate at one table, seated according to their birth order, Joseph sat at another table, and the Egyptians sat at a third table. When the portions were served, Benjamin's portion was five times as much as the brother's portion. Joseph continued to show favoritism to Benjamin, just as his father Jacob had shown toward Joseph himself years earlier. In those days, the brothers had been jealous, and Joseph wanted to see if jealousy still resided in their hearts. Would they isolate Benjamin from the fellowship at their table? The exact opposite occurred. They feasted with him. Joseph witnessed an interaction with the brothers and Benjamin that he had not had in Canaan.

Was the brothers' fellowship with Benjamin just for show, or was it sincere? This would be the third test. Before the brothers left for Canaan, Joseph commanded the house steward, saying, "Put my cup, the silver cup, in the mouth of the sack of the youngest, and his money for the grain."[175] As the brothers departed for home, they joined together probably in great relief. The brothers had tried to return the money from the first trip, reclaimed Simeon, and were on their way home with Benjamin and more grain for the family. Imagine their shock when Joseph's house steward caught up with

---

174 Genesis 43:23.

175 Genesis 44:2.

them and leveled an accusation of theft. Confidently, the brother's responded, "With whomever of your servants it is found, let him die, and we also will be my lord's slaves."[176] Imagine their surprise and horror to see the silver cup pulled from Benjamin's bag and, because of their response to the allegation, to realize the death sentence they had placed on Benjamin and the life of slavery placed on themselves.

Upon their return, Joseph offered his brothers the option of returning home in peace, but Benjamin had to remain behind and be his servant. The evidence seemed to be incriminating, and their personal escape ensured. Thus, this test would reveal their true feelings about their youngest brother. Then, Judah pleaded on the behalf of Benjamin. Judah told of the fondness Jacob and Benjamin had. He explained that Benjamin was the only one left from his mother, and that Jacob had despaired of allowing Benjamin to travel to Egypt in the first place. Judah shared his fear that returning home without Benjamin would lead to Jacob's death. His plea ended with his offering himself as a slave in the place of Benjamin.

Judah was the one who suggested the idea of selling Joseph into slavery. Joseph knew Judah as perverse and deceitful in those days; was he the same man? No, Judah was sincere in his love for a favorite brother as opposed to the man who twenty years before made a profit by selling the favorite brother into slavery. The servants were dismissed; thus, Joseph and his brothers were in the room alone. In an emotional confession, Joseph revealed, "I am your brother Joseph, whom you sold into Egypt."[177] The brothers were speechless; the same Joseph sold into slavery was second to Pharaoh.

---

176   Genesis 44:9.

177   Genesis 45:4.

Joseph informed them the famine would last for another five years. He encouraged them to tell their father, Jacob, that he was alive and that the family needed to move to Egypt. Pharaoh even provided the wagons and other provisions to move them.

One blessing of true reconciliation is that blessings can be shared. Joseph was able to reunite with his family. The heart of reconciliation desires to extend mercy and build up relationships that have been broken. Joseph made his brothers endure tests, but his heart behind the tests revealed a desire to reconcile. Joseph told his brothers three times in Genesis 45 that God was in control by sending him to Egypt; God sent Joseph to Egypt. This does not dismiss the brothers' sin, but Joseph saw God working in his life despite their sin.

Paul reiterated this thought in Romans. "And we know that God causes all things to work together for good to those who love God, to those who are called according to His purpose."[178] Therefore, Joseph encouraged them. "Do not quarrel on the journey."[179] Reconciliation is not a time for casting a false blessing or claiming personal victory. The heart of reconciliation is to glorify God because He restored something that was broken.

The years of lost fellowship could be rekindled, and God's grace continued because, "Now Israel lived in the land of Egypt, in Goshen, and they acquired property in it and were fruitful and became very numerous."[180] Biblical reconciliation is filled with many blessings. God blessed Potiphar's house while Joseph was there. God

---

178 Romans 8:28.

179 Genesis 45:24.

180 Genesis 47:27.

blessed Joseph in jail. God blessed Pharaoh through Joseph. God blessed Israel to have joy in the midst of a famine.

HOW DO I FORGIVE AND FORGET?

The greatest test for reconciliation was given to Joseph. Genesis 50 begins with Joseph weeping over Jacob's death. The brothers' weeping quickly turned to fear as they asked themselves, "What if Joseph bears a grudge against us and pays back in full for all the wrong which we did to him!" So they sent a message to Joseph, saying, "Your father charged before he died saying, "Thus you shall say to Joseph, "Please forgive, I beg you, the transgression of your brothers and their sin, for they did you wrong."[181] In theory, this would have been the perfect time to seek revenge. Joseph showered grace upon them while their father lived, but they feared that his grace indirectly blessed them. They could see no reason for Joseph to extend kindness to them after their father died.

Why does God continue to shower grace upon believers? There are times of frustration as we repeat the same sin as well as embarrassment in asking God's forgiveness once again. A fear similar to that of the brothers can be in the back of one's mind as well. Jeremiah 31 is a chapter of great hope because in it, God says, "For I will forgive their iniquity and their sin I will remember no more."[182] Elsewhere in Jeremiah, this theme is reiterated. "In those days and at that time, declares the Lord, search will be made for the iniquity of Israel, but there will be none; and for the sins of Judah, but they will not be found; for I will pardon those whom I leave

---

181 Genesis 50:15–17.

182 Jeremiah 31:34b.

as a remnant."[183] Capturing the vastness of God's forgiveness, the psalmist wrote, "As far as the east is from the west, so far has He removed our transgressions from us."[184] This is the answer to why believers should never fear that God will decide to void salvation. God forgets confessed sins.

There is a greater peace when one realizes why God will never void salvation. God's forgetfulness (Hebrew word, *zakar*) is a call to action. For example, God used this word to reprimand Israel. In rebellion, they were to remember God not because their minds forgot Him, but they forgot God in the sense that their actions were against Him. The problem of their "forgetfulness" focused upon their lifestyle choices more than their intellect. When *zakar* is applied to God, it signifies an implementation of His plan, not a lost memory; that is the context of Jeremiah 31:34, a progression of God's plan. When we take into account the mindset of Old Testament believers who knew they had to make a yearly sacrifice until Messiah came, we understand God's forgetfulness. God will remember our sin no more meant that the Messiah completed the work set before Him to satisfy God's wrath. God's forgetfulness was an action of unlimited grace to assure believers that His salvation is secure. There will be no point in time that God will even consider breaking His covenant of salvation. God took action, refusing to allow any condemnation to be brought against the believer because Christ has satisfied God's justice and judgment for the believer.

God's knowledge extends to knowing every detail of a man, from the number of hairs on his head to the deep intentions of his heart. If God can intellectually forget, that would alter the definition

---

183 Jeremiah 50:20.

184 Psalm 103:12.

of omniscience, which would place great concern on His certainty to lead believers on the pathway to holiness. It would also alter the definition of grace. Knowing every sin of the unbeliever, God extends grace every time He prompts the unbeliever to respond by faith to His salvation. Why, then, must God forget the sins of believers in order to keep His covenant with those He has already redeemed? The good news is that God gives grace because of His desire instead of what one deserves. Keep in mind that the Lord knows all the sins in the believer's past, present, and future, both confessed and unconfessed. Yet, He will never allow any sin to cancel a believer's salvation, and this is God showering more grace upon the believer.

In response to his brothers, Joseph said, "As for you, you meant evil against me, but God meant it for good in order to bring about this present result, to preserve many people alive. So therefore, do not be afraid; I will provide for you and your little ones."[185] Joseph spoke with compassion and great kindness. He realized that the sovereignty of God surpassed their sinful actions to accomplish a plan greater than Joseph or his brothers could ever imagine. This is the identity of reconciliation. Joseph had a chance to take revenge; instead, Joseph wept because they feared his forgiveness was not genuine. Joseph viewed the past through the eyes of forgiveness and reconciliation. Grace means there was no need to bring up confessed and forgiven sins!

The acts of extending forgiveness and walking the path of restoration are spiritual battles. Each discipline offers different challenges; nonetheless, the standard of holiness still applies. The way God extends forgiveness to the believer is that "while we were yet

---

185 Genesis 50:20–21.

sinners," and that must be the catalyst motivating and measuring the forgiveness from the believer. God's grace continuing to pour upon the believer with the blessings of restoration serves to model His willing heart as an example for His people to seek reconciliation.

Many mock God's forgiveness, restoration, and grace; however, the pursuit of God's ways leads to freedom. There is the freedom from bitterness, emotional outburst, and the trap of letting one sin multiply into more sins. God will supply the need for strength, perspective, and peace through His gracious gifts so that the believer is able to pursue His holiness. Peter encouraged believers, saying, "You therefore, beloved, knowing this beforehand, be on your guard so that you are not carried away by the error of unprincipled men and fall from your own steadfastness, but grow in the grace and knowledge of our Lord and Savior Jesus Christ. To Him be the glory, both now and to the day of eternity. Amen."[186] You may think you can accomplish this task, but I know He will accomplish His plan through the joyful surrender of your heart!

---

186 2 Peter 3:17–18.

Chapter 9

WHAT A VIEW

"OUTWARD MORALITY IS NOT ENOUGH for salvation. An inward change is necessary."[187] Jonathan Edward's plain statements rang thunderously through the ears to the hearts of many during the Great Awakening. His intolerance of lip service to the Lord prompted many sermons, such as *Sinners in the Hands of an Angry God*, intending to cut to an individual's heart, and they did. Scores of people repented from their self-serving religion and were converted to total dependency upon God's grace for salvation. Others reviled Edwards. He was relieved of his pastoral duties from his church in Northampton for his persistency that only those who made professions of faith could partake of the Lord's Supper.

Whether loved or loathed, Edwards' involvement in the Great Awakening is well documented. David Brainerd more than likely would have been forgotten if not for Edwards. Even though they probably knew each other only for five years, and the Edwards family cared for David during his last five months of life, David Brainerd, who died at the age of twenty-nine, made a valuable impression on the minister. Brainerd once recorded,

---

187 Jonathan Edwards, ed., *The Life and Diary of David Brainerd* (Peabody, MA: Hendrickson Publishers, 2006), ix.

I felt exceedingly calm, and quite resigned to God, respecting my future employment, when and where he pleased. My faith lifted me above the world, and removed all those mountains, that I could not look over of late. I wanted not the favor of man to lean upon; for I knew Christ's favor was infinitely better, and that it was no matter when, nor where, nor how Christ should send me, nor what trials he should still exercise me with, if I might be prepared for his work and will. I now found revived, in my mind, the wonderful discovery of infinite wisdom in all the dispensations of God towards me, which I had a little before I met with my great trial at college; every thing appeared full of divine wisdom.[188]

Brainerd died painfully, which is reminiscent of some trials he endured. He was wrongfully expelled from Yale, where he had studied in preparation for the ministry. This rejection carried severe consequences since it was nearly impossible to gain church employment without a seminary degree. From his journal entry, Brainerd's confidence in the Lord displays the reason Jonathan Edwards endeared himself to this young man, for he had such an elevated view of God and openly wrote about his personal struggles.

I fear that when discussing obedience to follow the Lord and the struggles encountered on the journey of faith, the blessings of following God are diminished. Brainerd set forth an example that even though one may face rejection, humiliation, and dire circumstances, the presence of the Lord establishes joy for the believer.

Within the contents of this book, trials and difficulties have

---

188 Ibid, 34-35.

been elaborated upon because every believer who desires to pursue the holiness of God will face such scenarios. Some of God's gracious provisions have also received attention, and this chapter continues that thought. Christ has called us to trade in temporary joys for an eternal joy that begins on the earth, and this chapter presents some of those joys.

RELATIONSHIP WITH GOD

"My faith lifted me above the world, and removed all those mountains, that I could not look over of late." Those words seemed to leap off the page when I laid eyes on that journal entry for the first time. I was excited and encouraged to read the testimony of one whose heart shined brightly despite his trials. To be fair, though, other journal entries contained his seasons of frustration and anxiety as Brainerd faced hardships. Such a roller coaster ride of emotions should not surprise or discourage the believer. The willingness to be that open and honest with God contradicted the religious piousness that Jonathan Edwards lamented. Pretentious religion does not walk far on the road of suffering and neither will it illuminate the greatness of salvation. During the last five months of Brainerd's life, Edwards was moved with respect and adoration for his young friend's desire to glorify God in life and death. The peace and joy that Edwards often mentioned in sermons was presented through David Brainerd.

With all the trials he endured, Brainerd's joy rested in understanding the great love of God. Paul affirmed,

> For the love of Christ controls us, having concluded this, that one died for all, therefore all died; and He died for all,

so that they who live might no longer live for themselves, but for Him who died and rose again on their behalf. Therefore from now on we recognize no one according to the flesh; even though we have known Christ according to the flesh, yet now we know Him in this way no longer. Therefore if anyone is in Christ, he is a new creature; the old things passed away; behold, new things have come.[189]

The key to experiencing God's joy intertwines with the love of Christ that controls us; a personal relationship with Jesus Christ changes everything. Without rehashing the whole book, think to some of the topics covered up to this point, such as yielding personal rights to God, enduring trials with godliness, accepting God's gifts, forgiving others, and desiring true restoration when possible. These commitments provide a few examples for the identity of God's holiness. Tozer clarified, "God's holiness is not simply the best we know infinitely bettered. We know nothing like the divine holiness. It stands apart, unique, unapproachable, incomprehensible and unattainable. The natural man is blind to it. He may fear God's power and admire His wisdom, but His holiness he cannot even imagine."[190] Since an unbeliever's understanding of God's holiness falls short, the ability to imitate the holiness of God extends no further than his understanding.

In the Garden of Eden, God entrusted Adam and Eve to rule the earth and its inhabitants. God blessed them with knowing Him and with the ability to reason with His ways so that they could fulfill the Lord's expectations. When they sinned in the Garden, however,

---

189 2 Corinthians 5:14–17.

190 A.W. Tozer, *The Knowledge of the Holy* (New York: HarperCollins, 1961), 104.

they created enmity between all humans and God to the extent that everybody is born without having a personal relationship with Him. Read the dire consequences as Paul lamented, "There is none righteous, not even one; there is none who understands, there is none who seeks for God; all have turned aside, together they have become useless; there is none who does good, there is not even one."[191] However, the earth still needs to be governed, and God still expects to have His holiness be the standard by which humanity governs the earth. But, since unbelievers are incapable of knowing God intimately, they have formulated their own philosophies and plans to rule the earth and its inhabitants. They replaced God's holy philosophy and plan with their own, and the Lord has called that idolatry. Enmity continues to exist due to the constant falling short of the life that can only be found in God's gift of salvation.

In the end, life apart from having a relationship with God will result in condemnation. Jonathan Edwards said, "The wrath of God burns against them, their damnation does not slumber; the pit is prepared, the fire is made ready, the furnace is now hot, ready to receive them; the flames do now rage and glow. The glittering sword is whet, and held over them, and the pit hath opened its mouth under them."[192] Every person deserves eternal condemnation because of the animosity man has toward God and his inability to know about God's holiness, much less maintain that purity. Yet, believers at one time were alienated from the knowledge and power of God needed to fulfill His plan.

Apart from God's grace, failure and discouragement are the end results of our best attempts. Commands in the Bible meet resentment

---

191 Romans 3:10–12.

192 Edwards, Sermons of Jonathan Edwards, 401–402.

when encountering someone attempting to be a good person in the sight of God. Pile upon that frustration the fact that the closer one is drawn to God, the more sin is revealed; then how can joy ever come out of pursuing the holiness of God when failures always occur? The answer is the love of Christ, which He has implanted within the hearts of those who place their faith in Him.

A right relationship with God controlling the believer filled with His love enables one to endure the journey set before him. When Paul wrote, "the love of Christ controls us," he knew the standards of God and the hearts of even believers at times want to walk different paths. Believers struggle with yielding rights, forgiving, and all the other standards of God; unfortunately, I know this because of experience. Every step toward spiritual maturity leads to a revelation of many areas that conflict with God's holiness; why continue down the road of maturity when one can settle for the status quo? Paul's usage of the word *control* describes a pressure that produces another action. The reason I desire to walk God's path is only because of the love that Christ has placed in my heart, which is sealed by His Spirit. A right relationship with God produces the fire in believers to walk the path the Lord has prepared and to walk it with joy.

To some, the oddity is that freedom in Christ means that I surrender to Christ in order to fulfill His plan. Yet, that surrender brings an everlasting and meaningful joy because I can then view God differently. Remember, "He died for all, so that they who live might no longer live for themselves, but for Him who died and rose again on their behalf." The glad surrender to God embraces the knowledge that the Lord not only gives pleasurable gifts to believers, but that He is our greatest gift of pleasure. No gift of equal—much less greater—value compares to God's presence. Resist the temptation to think that God changing everything around you will provide peace; His presence is peace. The love of Christ compels the heart of those who trust in Him to joyfully absorb the blessing of His presence.

Furthermore, the love of Christ controls believers to view others and ourselves differently. Paul said, "Therefore from now on we recognize no one according to the flesh ... Therefore if anyone is in Christ, he is a new creature; the old things passed away; behold, new things have come." Believers should think more highly of others and less of themselves; unfortunately, some believers think more highly of themselves and less of others.

In an earlier letter to the Corinthian church, Paul used the imagery of a physical body to teach truths about the spiritual body, the local church. The summary of his teaching is this: "And if one member suffers, all the members suffer with it; if one member is honored, all the members rejoice with it. Now you are Christ's body, and individually members of it."[193] The unity of the church goes beyond common beliefs and extends to a common love from which Christ loved us first. Paul's instruction that "we recognize no one according to the flesh" emphasizes an open dialogue received by an interested listener. He taught the church to know one another beyond the outward appearance so that we can specifically pray for each other.

Invest time developing a spiritual bond with another believer for the benefit of having a prayer or accountability partner. Since we are to exhort, rebuke, and reprove each other unto righteousness, utilize God's grace as a means to encourage another

---

193 1 Corinthians 12:26–27.

believer in the journey to pursue God's holiness. I have often heard it rightly said that God's grace meets us where we are, but do not fail to recognize that God's love takes that same person down the path of holiness. God desires for His people to be active participants in His kingdom. To the church in Ephesus, Paul instructed,

> And He gave some as apostles, and some as prophets, and some as evangelists, and some as pastors and teachers, for the equipping of the saints for the work of service, to the building up of the body of Christ; until we all attain to the unity of the faith, and of the knowledge of the Son of God, to a mature man, to the measure of the stature which belongs to the fullness of Christ.[194]

Do not misunderstand Paul by thinking that those responsibilities entirely belong to the staff of a church. He gave the church ministers to be catalysts for others to follow their example until all members of the church unify in service and sanctification; by the way, there will always be work in those fields. Yet, it is the love of Christ that controls us to pursue that goal with joy.

REASON WITH GOD

If a mind could retain every description of God's holiness time itself could not even provide enough opportunities to digest His fullness. Humbly, Paul observed, "Oh, the depth of the riches both of the wisdom and knowledge of God! How unsearchable are His judgments and unfathomable His ways."[195] Isaiah explained, "For as

---

194 Ephesians 4:11–13.

195 Romans 11:33.

the heavens are higher than the earth, so are My ways higher than your ways and My thoughts than your thoughts."[196]

Graciously, God sealed His work of salvation before the foundations of the heavens and the earth. Luck had nothing to do with God's plan for you; grace, mercy, and love flowing from God were provided for your need to respond properly to Him. In other words, God implanted His Spirit in believers to create and sustain a longing to know God and His holiness more intimately. The pursuit to discover God can never be exhausted, but an exhilarating journey awaits those who are led through the depths of His understanding. As a result, this pursuit is the discovery of the believer's identity in Christ, which produces humility and awe concerning the greatness of God and His ways.

Paul wrote, "And we know that God causes all things to work together for good to those who love God, to those who are called according to His purpose."[197] The following testimony comes from a godly believer who wanted to remain anonymous, which does not surprise me. Her dedication to glorify the Lord radiates through her actions and words even when the "all things" described by Paul contain difficulties. She entitled this testimony, "Mine Is a Story of Faith":

> Mine is a story of faith, of grace, of God-ordained trials. My short thirty years of life have not been what I had planned or anticipated. They have been full of difficult seasons, but they were by His sovereignty designed for me, not just to endure, but to endure with a heart that would please the Designer.

---

196 Isaiah 55:9.

197 Romans 8:28.

God saved me when I was fifteen years old. I had grown up in the church and had heard the gospel hundreds of times, but God opened my ears to "hear" it in a way that would change my life forever one Wednesday night in 1996. I was convicted of my sin and repented as honestly as I knew how. I surrendered my life to Jesus and committed to do what He wanted me to do, whatever that entailed, for the rest of my life.

God allowed me to be involved with several ministries during my teenage and young adult years. I worked with children and teenagers in various settings, and I loved every opportunity. What an honor it is for God to allow us to be a part of His eternal business! I had several good teachers during these years who taught me what it looked like to love God with my whole heart and how to study God's Word, not to find verses that benefited me, but to study verse by verse, chapter by chapter to discover what God was saying through His Scriptures. God was laying a foundation of faith that He knew I would heavily rely on in the coming years.

As a freshman in college, I continued to grow in my faith. I was challenged toward maturity in Christ by Bible study, books, and new friends. I was doing well in school and adjusting to college life quickly. I was so happy! Then one day, with no warning, I began to notice slight changes in the coordination of my fingers. I began having difficulty managing small things; I dropped things more and more often. This was odd because I had never had any trouble like this before. Three months later, I began to stumble and fall for no reason. I walked around campus for exercise often early in the morning before classes started; these walks were becoming dangerous because I would trip and fall so easily.

Soon, the lack of coordination in my hands and legs became a regular problem, and I saw a neurologist. He ran test after test but could find nothing. For four months, I was poked and prodded, all the while wondering what was happening because I was getting worse, and my doctor could tell me nothing. I was at college finishing my first year during all of this. I was scared. I knew something serious was happening to my body, and it was not going away. I cried out to God for help, for healing, for comfort. He answered. He showed me in His Word how powerful and sovereign He was, He gave me faith to believe I could trust Him to take care of me, and He took away my fear. I was still very unsure about my future and what would unfold, but I had every confidence that my God would not let me walk this path alone and without an eternal purpose.

My health slowly worsened over the following months; God was faithful to lead me as I had decisions to make about continuing school. My needs were changing as my walking and daily activities became more difficult. But it was clear that God intended for me to continue school because of His guidance and the provisions He made. He provided multiple motorized scooters, extra money, and specific accommodations that normally required lots of time and red tape. All of these things were given to me in a matter of hours and days rather than months. My parents and I were seeking the Lord's direction, and He was faithful to direct. I was confident I was doing just what God wanted me to do.

After four years of school, I still had no idea what was causing my health problems. I had, by this time, had second opinions but no answers from doctors. I had great difficulty walking even short distances without falling because my balance was so poor, so I used a walker and a motorized scooter to get around. I graduated with my bachelor's degree in speech-language pathology in May 2007. I was so excited! In spite of the additional hardships I had been given, I was accomplishing what God had set before me.

I came home for the summer and after a few weeks, my dad sat me down and told me he was moving out and divorcing my mom. I was blind-sided with this news and was completely devastated. My family had always been so important to me; they were my foundation. I felt confused, hurt, betrayed. I cried out to God again to help me, to comfort my soul, and to heal my broken heart. Again, He answered.

I returned to college in the fall to start graduate school. I prayed a lot. Graduate school is hard and stressful on its own, let alone adding to it a serious, undiagnosed, progressive neurological condition and a recent, overwhelming divorce. Suffice it to say, I did not know which end was up most days. But, I continued to seek the Lord; He continued to give me grace to handle my trials and the faith to trust Him. I was lying in bed one night ready to go to sleep, and I found myself smiling ... for no reason. I remembered doing that often during those hard days and weeks, and I wondered why. I asked God, "Why am I smiling? My world is literally falling to pieces around me. I can't walk from here to there without falling; my family is an absolute wreck; I'm so stressed about deadlines and coursework and clinical … and I'm lying here with a smile on my face. How am I okay? Why?" I really wanted to know, so I laid there in silence, hoping for an answer. After a minute or two passed, Philippians 4:6–7 came to mind. "Be anxious for nothing, but in everything by prayer and supplication with thanksgiving let your requests be made known to God. And the peace of God, which surpasses all comprehension, will guard your hearts and your minds in Christ Jesus." That was it!! That was why I was okay. God's peace—which I cannot understand—was actually standing guard over my mind and heart because I had earnestly prayed and prayed and prayed. I love it when God takes time to answer my questions, no matter how unimportant they are in the grand scheme of things. He is so patient with us; I am so grateful!

I graduated with my master's degree six semesters later. By this time, God had given me a van, a motorized wheelchair, and a lift to put the chair in and out of the vehicle. I was praying, and God was leading and providing. I did not know where, but I was confident God had a job already lined up for me. Sure enough, I waited until God said to "go," and I went and was hired during my first interview. God has faithfully and thoroughly taken care of the details of my life since the moment He called me to Himself. I am so glad He calls me His own.

I work at a local hospital as the speech pathologist. God uses my wheelchair to start conversations with perfect strangers on a weekly basis. Patients and visitors to the hospital ask me very often about my condition. I never considered how odd it would be for them to work with a professional in a wheelchair. Nor did I ever realize how bold they could be in asking very personal and sometimes inappropriate questions like, "You work here in a hospital and you're in that?" (pointing to my wheelchair). I smile and answer without divulging personal information. After further questions, they always say, "Well, honey, I'm so sorry this has happened to you." I often say, "I'm not. I'm fine. I surrendered my life to God when I was fifteen years old. I believe that this, for whatever reason, is part of His plan for me. How about you?"

My health will likely never be restored unless God chooses to heal me. And because of His peace, I am okay with that. My family, as I knew it, will likely never be the same. And because of His peace, I am okay with that as well. My trials have not ended; there are likely many more to come. And because of His peace, I already know that I will be okay.

I remember joining others to pray for this dear friend and fellow servant of the Lord, that she would be able to walk in the manner she was formerly accustomed to. At the writing of this chapter, she still depends upon a wheelchair for mobility, but the other prayer request—and to her, the most important request—has been answered abundantly. Her faith in the Lord has grown beyond measure as her reasoning with God and His ways found joy and contentment in the Lord's grace. She has embraced this difficulty for the purposes of praising the Lord, and her knowledge and intimacy with Him challenges others to practice this type of submissiveness. Although her body is confined to a motorized wheelchair, she is captivated by the Lord.

REPRESENT GOD

Imagine that the nation you love is in chaos due to the lack of leadership because the man who reigned over the country for fifty-two years died. During the last part of his reign, pride in his heart convinced him to burn incense on the altar, despite being prohibited from this activity by the Lord. Thus, God struck King Uzziah with leprosy, and he died a leper cut off from the house of the Lord. Uncertainty in leadership caused anxiety and made Israel vulnerable to their neighboring enemies. Assyria had conquered the northern kingdom of Israel, and Judah, the southern kingdom, felt threatened.

Despite his indiscretion, King Uzziah did right in the sight of the Lord, and the Lord prospered him and the kingdom. Nonetheless, there was little consolation due to the increasing moral decay the country was experiencing. As the prophet of the Lord, Isaiah was concerned about Judah's need for another godly king. Isaiah and others feared that an ungodly king would lead people away from the Lord. These matters weighed heavily upon the prophet's heart, and this description serves as a backdrop to Isaiah 6. It is written,

> In the year of King Uzziah's death I saw the Lord sitting on a throne, lofty and exalted, with the train of His robe filling the temple. Seraphim stood above Him … And one called out to another and said, "Holy, Holy, Holy, is the Lord of hosts, the whole earth is full of His glory." And the foundations of the thresholds trembled at the voice of him who called out, while the temple was filling with smoke.[198]

---

198 Isaiah 6:1–4.

Isaiah was rightfully concerned about the identity and character of the next king for Judah; instead, he saw the identity and character of the King over all creation.

This opportunity was the perfect time to request that God raise up a godly king quickly. Yet, observe Isaiah's greatest concern standing before God, "Woe is me, for I ruined! Because I am a man of unclean lips, and I live among a people of unclean lips; for my eyes have seen the King, the Lord of hosts."[199] Judah still was without a king, and Isaiah still had deep concerns; so, why did Isaiah respond that way when he stood in the presence of God? Isaiah's view of God changed drastically, even though the problems and concerns did not change. He stood there in need of a divine cleansing, and that is what God gave him. It is written, "Then one of the seraphim flew to me with a burning coal in his hand, which he had taken from the altar with tongs. He touched my mouth with it and said, 'Behold, this has touched your lips; and your iniquity is taken away and your sin is forgiven.'"[200] To the glory of God, Isaiah, who although once tainted by unclean lips, had his inadequacies exchanged to have peace with God. Graciously, God gave the prophet all he needed to be cleansed.

The fear of combating neighboring kings melted when Isaiah pondered how he or anyone could stand before a holy God. The Lord's presence amazed Isaiah; in addition, God's request excited the prophet. It is written, "Then I heard the voice of the Lord, saying, 'Whom shall I send, and who will go for

---

199 Isaiah 6:5.

200 Isaiah 6:6–7.

Us?' Then I said, 'Here am I. Send me!'"[201] Heaven's nominating committee did not have to negotiate the terms of how this opportunity would benefit Isaiah, nor did they offer a front row parking space next to the awning. Isaiah bypassed any attempts to negotiate with God because his eyes were fixated on the King of all creation; thus, joy compelled his commitment. A proper view of God results in the desire to represent God before the people; God has a heart to tell people about the gospel. Since he was cleansed by God's grace, the prophet did not think twice about the great privilege to speak on behalf of the One who blessed him. The Lord expects the benefactors of His grace to proclaim His message to a world in need of Him; reasonably, Isaiah's response passionately asked for the Lord to send him.

Since God is so great, He deserves to be worshipped by all people, and His Word demands that the gospel be spoken to every person. God's desire for believers to participate in the proclamation of His Word still astonishes my mind since He is perfect, and I am very much flawed. At times, my mind wanders to the derogatory comments others have made, questioning God's call for me to pastor or even to preach. Those critics are correct because I am not worthy of this calling; however, if anyone thinks they are worthy to speak or work on behalf of the Lord, they are wrong. There is a familiar saying, "God does not call the equipped; He equips the called." Joy in serving God flows from the heart that recognizes God's commitment to lead and strengthen believers.

The excitement of the prophet ignited a passion to go to any place and to preach any message. To some, Isaiah's commitment and joy to participate in God's work ends God's expectations. On

---
201 Isaiah 6:8.

the contrary, the conversation continued as follows:

> [God] said, "Go, and tell this people: keep on listening, but do not perceive; keep on looking, but do not understand. Render the hearts of this people insensitive, their ears dull, and their eyes dim, otherwise they might see with their eyes, hear with their ears, understand with their hearts, and return and be healed." Then I said, "Lord, how long?" And he answered, "Until cities are devastated and without inhabitant, houses are without people and the land is utterly desolate, The Lord has removed men far away, and the forsaken places are many in the midst of the land. Yet there will be a tenth portion in it, and it will again be subject to burning, like a terebinth or an oak whose stump remains when it is felled. The holy seed is its stump.[202]

This type of response by the people did not meet Isaiah's expectations, and in the middle of this passage, he asked, "Lord, how long?" Isaiah became disheartened when he heard the news that the people would reject God's Word.

There is no delight when people reject the gospel, especially if that rejection persists to the moment of death. Anguish and grief on behalf of those souls should intensify the church's prayer life, both individually and collectively. Heartache beyond description grips the hearts of many believers who invest time in evangelism and discipleship, disciplines involving all believers, not just the staff of a church. If God's love resides in someone, how can that person be unaffected by the spiritual vacancies of the people around them? The prophet feared for the people who ignored God's warnings and

---

202 Isaiah 6:9–13.

whose wrath would soon prevail against them.

Isaiah was compelled to preach to people whom the Lord said would not listen; nonetheless, he was commissioned to proclaim God's truth. It would seem that joy cannot be found when people do not respond by faith to God's message, but that would be a mistaken notion. Although there is no joy in their rejection, there is joy when the purity of God's message is presented despite the way people respond to the gospel. When the apostles were mistreated for sharing the gospel, they were strictly warned to stop preaching. They were tormented, ridiculed, and marked as dangerous by the religious enemies to Christ. It is written, "So they went on their way from the presence of the Council, rejoicing that they had been considered worthy to suffer shame for His name. And every day, in the temple and from house to house, they kept right on teaching and preaching Jesus as the Christ."[203] These men found joy in Christ during injustices and merciless treatment, just as Isaiah did years earlier.

One reason that Isaiah and the apostles had joy despite knowing they would suffer was because God entrusted His message to them. Viewing God properly will increase one's commitment to God; in the same manner, knowing that God entrusts believers as they experience difficulties to glorify Him should change the way believers view trials. As hard as they are, trials provide opportunities to demonstrate faith in the Lord, and that is all that one needs to have joy. The apostles rejoiced because the Lord considered them worthy to suffer for Him. As for Isaiah, he preached to people who couldn't care less about God. He had to recognize the source of true joy comes through obedience to the Lord. The message of this

---

[203] Acts 5:41–42.

book centers around discovering peace and joy that comes from a fellowship with God. This type of joy and peace does not waver on public opinion; rather, it is based upon righteousness, holiness, and faithfulness. Only the Lord can be the author and sustainer of something so wonderful.

Another reason that they had joy and peace was the assurance that God would produce His fruit through them. To Isaiah, the Lord said, "The Lord has removed men far away, and the forsaken places are many in the midst of the land."[204] This meant that God's judgment upon the people would be very severe, and it was filled with utter devastation. In the midst of His judgments and corrections, there is always a concern that God will forsake His promises or His people. The Lord continued, "Yet there will be a tenth portion in it, and it will again be subject to burning, like a terebinth or an oak whose stump remains when it is felled. The holy seed is its stump."[205] Despite the destruction they saw, God reminded the people that He was at work even though they could not see His fruit and even when they doubted His plan. God was at work, and He accomplished His plan to prune His people as He works to prune His people today. The Lord would use the great punishment that He executed. Without justifying their sin, the Lord used the brothers' actions of selling Joseph into slavery, false imprisonments, and even a forgetful chief cupbearer to accomplish His will. Place your faith in the Almighty by trusting that everything you enjoy and endure is all for the glory of God. Then you will see that God worked in your life to not only bless you but also grow you into maturity, to count you worthy to represent Him no matter the

---

204 Isaiah 6:12.

205 Isaiah 6:13.

circumstance. His purpose is to "Consecrate yourselves therefore, and be holy, for I am holy."[206] As Joseph told his brothers, "As for you, you meant evil against me, but God meant it for good in order to bring about this present result, to preserve many people alive."[207] This is joy; this is ministry; this is a view of God that will lead you down his glorious path.

---

[206] Leviticus 11:44.

[207] Genesis 50:20.

Chapter 10
WHY ME?

EXCITEMENT FROM SPREADING THE GOSPEL of Jesus Christ in El Salvador helped me fight the exhaustion of a week of long days and the flight back home. I was entrusted with the responsibility of leading group devotions every morning, but I am not a morning person. Shortly after the devotions, we loaded into the van and traveled to a church to minister to the people of the community. It was a pure delight to see different places and share the gospel with people who needed to hear the Good News.

Whatever can be said about traveling to different places, I tend to agree with the adage, "There is no place like home." I looked forward to walking into my kitchen so that I could make some sweet tea and catch up on the football scores from that day, November 9, 2002. Specifically, I was interested in the LSU game played at Kentucky. I found a game that was almost at halftime, so I figured that would be the best way to see the score or possibly a highlight from the game. Since the game was not highly profiled, I was surprised to hear the announcers talk about the "Bluegrass Miracle." LSU was favored to win; therefore, I braced myself to hear the news that LSU lost.

Highlights from the game came on after a few minutes of advertisements, and I leaned back in my chair. LSU had a lead by as many as fourteen points and was ahead by ten points in the fourth quarter. Then, they showed how Kentucky made a furious comeback and even took a 30-27 lead with eleven seconds on the clock. LSU was pinned down on their own nine-yard line when they completed a seventeen-yard pass. They were seventy-four yards away from the end zone with two seconds remaining on the clock. Fans started gathering on the field, and Kentucky head football coach Guy Morriss received a Gatorade bath from his team before the last play. LSU Quarterback Marcus Randall threw the ball as far as he could. Filled with excitement, Kentucky fans rushed the field. Their excitement, however, turned into disappointment when they realized LSU Wide Receiver Devery Henderson caught the ball off a deflection and ran for a touchdown. Oddly enough, when Henderson crossed the end zone, the Jefferson Pilot Sports broadcast accidentally posted "Kentucky 30, LSU 27-FINAL." LSU won the game 33-30, and that is what is known as the "Bluegrass Miracle." Congratulations! You have made it to the last chapter of the book, and the end is near. From the beginning of this study of the life of Joseph, my desire has been to help those struggling with trials. For some, the rising of the sun in the eastern sky is met with fear, brokenness, or depression. You may even have trouble making sense of some of the events you have endured. The testimonies in this book verify that you are not alone. Included were some remarkable accounts of believers who faced fierce trials. Their struggles differed from one another, just as your struggles and mine differ. Trusting God to lead, strengthen, and encourage you is always the right solution, no matter the trial. Prayerfully, this book will be an encouraging resource for you to consult and share with others in the days ahead.

Before all the celebrations begin, I want to provide one word of caution. Although these lessons have definitely blessed my life, they need to be reaffirmed constantly to the mind. Unfortunately, I concur with the lamentations of Paul, who confessed, "For I know that nothing good dwells in me, that is, in my flesh; for the willing is present in me, but the doing of good is not. For the good that I want, I do not do, but I practice the very evil that I do not want."[208] You might as well label me "guilty as charged" when it comes to knowing something is sinful yet being selfish enough to sin. I get so disgusted with myself when I commit sins over and over and over and—well, you get the point! God's expectations for His people are that we "Consecrate yourselves therefore, and be holy, for I am holy."[209] I feel ashamed because of the presence of my sin, and I feel inadequate to stand before Him since His expectations will not change. What can we do? If you have similar fears, this chapter is for you.

HIS PROMISE OF PEACE

In the pursuit of holiness, the believer will sin many times. Problems with selfishness, pride, greed, lust, and other sins fought in the past will continue as a hindrance. Since God hates sin, what would prohibit the Lord from unleashing His wrath on His people? Paul exhorted, "Therefore, having been justified by faith, we have peace with God through our Lord Jesus Christ, through whom also we have access by faith into this grace in which we stand, and we

---

208 Romans 7:18–19.

209 Leviticus 11:44.

rejoice in hope of the glory of God."[210]

In the Garden of Gethsemane, when Jesus sweated drops of blood, He understood the cost needed so that believers can have peace with God. It was in the Garden that Jesus' allegiance to God's plan was manifested beyond comprehension. The day of judgment arrived, and the burden of sin was placed upon Him. As an innocent sacrifice, Jesus had to bear the identity of sin. He had to bear that which He detested with every fiber of His being. Jesus was the Person, and Calvary was the place where all the defilement rested. As evidenced by the sweat drops of blood, He grappled with the dreadful moments for which He had been sent.

God's righteousness demanded a total destruction of the rebellion waged against Him because of sin. The Lord could neither allow sin to go unpunished nor tolerate the taunting of His perfect plan to persist. Thus, God took the most definitive and holy action possible, the crucifixion. God "was pleased to crush Him, putting Him to grief."[211] Notice that God the Father was the One to crush His Son and to put Him to grief. It was not the Jews, the Romans, or even Satan that put Jesus on the cross. It was not the deceitfulness of Judas Iscariot that placed Jesus on the cross. The cross was a deliberate act of a holy God judging sin. The cross was God's plan before the foundations of the heavens and the earth, and no man or spiritual being stopped Him from fulfilling His plan.

While on the cross, Jesus cried out, "My God, My God, why have You forsaken Me?"[212] These words echoed loudly throughout

---

210 Romans 5:1–2. New King James Version.

211 Isaiah 53:10.

212 Matthew 27:46.

all creation; thus, there can be no tiptoeing around this statement. Jesus was not delirious, and neither did He misspeak. When Christ took upon Himself the identity of sin and became God's sinless sacrifice, the fullness of God's wrath was poured out and had to be endured. At the cross, the seriousness of God to righteously deal with sin occurred, while the commitment of God to uphold His righteousness was also testified. It was His only Son on the cross! God's fury and relentless wrath could be better understood with human reasoning if it had been one of us on that cross. If God's wrath was poured out on the guilty individuals, that would make sense; we would know that they got what they deserved. Instead, God poured out His wrath on the sinless Christ. Jesus completed the task of satisfying the wrath and righteousness of God. Words filled with honey's sweetness came from Jesus' mouth: "It is finished!"[213] Christ endured God's wrath so that believers could have peace with Him.

HIS INVITATION TO INTIMACY

You wake up excited because the day begins the start of a new job, a fresh start that was needed for a long time. Fellow employees express warmth and seem to care when they laugh at most of your jokes or ask questions with an interest in your answers. Certainly, this kind of environment was lacking at your former place of employment.

You are teamed up to follow and observe the employee who has won "Employee of the Month" twenty months and counting. With ease and brevity, highlights are presented of everything from the history of the company to those who are about

---
213 John 19:30.

to be history with the company. Time for a break cannot come soon enough as your head is about to explode. Millions of questions circulate in your mind, and fellow employees welcome any questions you have—at least, for now. You fear the coming time when the newness wears off and your faults are revealed. How will these coworkers respond then?

God's invitation to join His family is a great blessing! Nonetheless, uncertainty may resonate in your heart; perhaps to you, peace is known as only a temporary status. Every relationship or endeavor seems to end up at the same old place, no matter how nice it was in the beginning. Some may wonder if God's peace is the same scenario of having high expectations crash into cold reality. Can a flawed human being truly have peace with God? We may rationalize that since God hates sin, one day He will draw the line after we commit a certain number of sins. Once again, consider this: "Therefore, having been justified by faith, we have peace with God through our Lord Jesus Christ, through whom also we have access by faith into this grace in which we stand, and rejoice in hope of the glory of God."[214]

Continuing the thought of the peace God grants believers through faith, Paul used the words access and stand. A wise pastor once said, "There are some people who brighten the atmosphere when they walk into the room, while others brighten it when they walk out of the room." That second one is the person whose voice causes stomach pains and cold shivers down your back when you hear it. For the sake of appearance and perhaps civility, you can put up a good front for a few minutes of shallow conversation. With such an individual, peace is getting through

---

214 Romans 5:1–2 NKJV.

a conversation without going insane. Peace is enhanced by the distance placed between you and that person.

God's peace granted to believers is quite different because of the words access and stand. Concerning access, the meaning is to bring near, while the word stand refers to a permanent position. In other words, God's purpose in granting peace is to have an intimate relationship with His people throughout eternity. A genuine faith in Jesus Christ transfers believers from being enemies of God to being in the family of God.

Having personal access to God, being invited to approach Him personally, was a foreign concept to believers in the Old Testament. The high priests offered sacrifices for themselves and for God's chosen people, Israel. Yet, the priests' access to God was limited as well. God told Moses, "Tell your brother Aaron that he shall not enter at any time into the holy place inside the veil, before the mercy seat which is on the ark, or he will die; for I will appear in the cloud over the mercy seat."[215] Only on the Day of Atonement could the high priest go beyond the veil on behalf of the people. That was the only time a high priest could approach the holy place of God.

Yet, it is written, "Therefore let us draw near with confidence to the throne of grace, so that we may receive mercy and find grace to help in time of need."[216] I can only imagine the thoughts in the minds of Jewish believers in the first century hearing this statement for the first time. It was unthinkable to approach God if you were not the high priest and it was not the Day of Atonement. Death was certain for those people; so, how

---

215 Leviticus 16:2.

216 Hebrews 4:16.

could they approach the throne of grace with confidence? The answer is because Jesus is our High Priest; thus, believers have access to God.

Since Jesus is God, "we have access by faith into this grace in which we stand." The word stand refers to a permanent position. Christ has not only ushered believers into peace with God, but He has also secured that position eternally. The peace granted to believers by God was an act of grace accomplished by God. He wants you to seek Him with all your heart, soul, mind, and strength. Embrace intimacy with God by being honest with yourself and with Him in your prayer life. There is no need to convince God to love you more. When God pours more gifts of grace on you, realize that it is His natural character to provide for His people. He is simply amazing!

There are prayers on behalf of every believer that ask the Father to shower them with His grace. It is written, "Therefore He is able also to save forever those who draw near to God through Him, since He always lives to make intercession for them."[217] Also, it confirms, "In the same way the Spirit also helps our weakness; for we do not know how to pray as we should, but the Spirit Himself intercedes for us with groanings too deep for words; and He who searches the hearts knows what the mind of the Spirit is, because He intercedes for the saints according to the will of God."[218] You will not find better prayer warriors than the Son of God and the Spirit of God! Open the depths of your soul to the Lord and yield to His desire to have an intimate relationship.

---

217 Hebrews 7:25.

218 Romans 8:26–27.

HIS DELIGHT IN OUR DISCOVERY

As he gazed into the star-filled sky, Abraham heard the Lord say, "Now look toward the heavens, and count the stars, if you are able to count them ... So shall your descendants be."[219] Before a child was given to the aged couple, God promised descendants outnumbering the stars. To the naked eye, Abraham could not see all the stars that God created; yet, God knows the number and ensured Abraham that his descendants would outnumber them. Wisely, Abraham "believed in the LORD; and He reckoned it to him as righteousness."[220] Nonetheless, it would be years before Abraham was given the promised son.

In Romans 5, Paul continued, "and we exult in hope of the glory of God. And not only this, but we also exult in our tribulations, knowing that tribulation brings about perseverance; and perseverance, proven character; and proven character, hope; and hope does not disappoint, because the love of God has been poured out within our hearts through the Holy Spirit who was given to us."[221]

Keep in mind that Paul's line of thought is still tied to believers having peace with God. They have been given total access through Jesus Christ to confidently approach the throne of God. Such provisions justify the joy and praise from believers. Yet, God expects that same joy and praise to be present when believers endure tribulations. The reason can be found within a proper understanding that "hope does not disappoint."

In our culture, the word hope is associated with wishful thinking,

---

219 Genesis 15:5.

220 Genesis 15:6.

221 Romans 5:2b–5.

but that is far from the meaning of elpis. This Greek word describes a confident expectation of fulfillment. Concerning tribulations, hope is the confident expectation that God will use the hardship to fulfill His plan. Likewise, this hope will not disappoint or "bring shame, or to humiliate." Since expressing joy and praise during tribulation is unusual, there are critics that claim one's faith in God is useless or even idiotic. God promises that in the day that His work is complete, those who trust in Him will not be disappointed.

God knew how many stars filled the heavens when He promised Abraham descendants that would outnumber the stars. God knows how He will work through your life despite your tribulations. Just as Abraham discovered, it is wise and beneficial for us to trust God. The benefits of depending upon Him include the future ramifications, but there are benefits that can be experienced in the present day as well. God has provided opportunities for us to discover evidence that proves depending upon Him brings blessings our way.

Tribulation brings about perseverance. Despite persistent tribulations, depending upon God enables the believer to abide underneath the pressure. In essence, perseverance means that the believer learns from the Lord in the midst of tribulation, just as Joseph exemplified. Even as a slave and later a prisoner, he persevered to the point that he earned the trust of Potiphar and the chief jailor, and clearly learned how to be a good leader. Despite being sold into slavery and falsely accused, Joseph demonstrated character that honored God. He did not have to wait for the tribulations to end to discover that the Lord is good and faithful. Even though He used other people, the Lord provided Joseph with the encouragement, resources, and direction to accomplish His plan.

Perseverance brings about proven character, which speaks of enduring a trial whose outcome produces an authentic validation. The imagery that best describes "proven character" is the process of purifying metals. As metal is placed into fire, the impurities attached to the metal are not able to stand the heat; thus, the impurities detach. All that is left is the pure metal. Likewise, perseverance tests people to their core philosophies; if those beliefs fail to imitate God's character under pressure, they are exposed as false. The person is left with the stabilizing truth that endured the fire and was found to be an authentic belief.

Proven character brings about hope. To his brothers, Joseph confirmed, "As for you, you meant evil against me, but God meant it for good in order to bring about this present result, to preserve many people alive. So therefore, do not be afraid; I will provide for you and your little ones."[222] Joseph realized that God accomplished much more through the trials than teaching him how to endure hardships. He learned how to walk with God and experience God's peace in the midst of trials. Hope brings about decisions with no regrets.

CONCLUSION

There are times in my study when I sit back in my chair and just say, "Wow!" God amazes me! After sitting under knowledgeable teachers and pouring my heart into personal studies of the Bible, I am still learning new truths or new depths of truths I already know such as grace. God humbles me because with each new insight lies multiple facts about God that I had not considered.

No matter how long or deeply one has studied the Bible, every

---

222 Genesis 50:20–21.

maturing believer lives a life of discovery and confession. In fact, discovery of truth and confession of sin frequently accompany each other. To illustrate this relationship, consider the impact of having a light dimmer in a bedroom. Walking into the bedroom, you turn the light on to the dimmest output of light so that all you see is a darkened room with objects that are barely visible. There is enough light to see the bed, drawers, and other main pieces of furniture. Next, you brighten the light so that you see clothes on the floor and the junk mail scattered across the top of the entertainment center. Finally, you set the light to maximum output, which enables you to see dust on the furniture. The brighter the light, the more you discover how messy the room truly is.

Likewise, the discovery of biblical truth enables us to understand the holiness of God. An intimate relationship with God increases our awareness of how much of a mess our lives are in without Him. As a result, the discovery of biblical truth leads toward the need to confess more sin to God. It is not that biblical truth leads us to more sin; rather, the discovery of biblical truth makes us aware of sins that once were hidden from us. Whether aware or unaware, sin still poisons our minds and pollutes out hearts. The only reasonable response to God is for us to be dependent upon Him to cleanse us. Do not be afraid to allow God to introduce you to His holiness and to the depth of your sin. Trust Him during these times of exploration because He is doing something greater than revealing your sin. God is introducing you to His grace!

I think back to the eternal punishment that I rightly deserve but see Him render unto me His righteousness. Why me? I think back to my heart's foolish attempts to negotiate with God but see His mercy extended instead. Why me? I recognize all the sins that I commit against Him, yet His Son and His Spirit faithfully intercede on my behalf, and I think, "Why me?" I end this book with the meaning of the title, Why Me? Paul clarified,

> Oh, the depth of the riches both of the wisdom and knowledge of God! How unsearchable are His judgments and unfathomable His ways! For who has known the mind of the Lord, or who became His counselor? Or who has first given to Him that it might be paid back to Him again? For from Him and through Him and to Him are all things. To Him be the glory forever. Amen. Therefore I urge you, brethren, by the mercies of God, to present your bodies a living and holy sacrifice, acceptable to God, which is your spiritual service of worship. And do not be conformed to this world, but be transformed by the renewing of your mind, so that you may prove what the will of God is, that which is good and acceptable and perfect. For through the grace given to me I say to everyone among you not to think more highly of himself than he ought to think; but to think so as to have sound judgment, as God has allotted to each a measure of faith.[223]

Blessings to you, and may God be exalted in all the earth!

Humbly His,
Kenny

---

[223] Romans 11:33–12:3.

For more information about
Kenneth D. Moore
&
WHY ME?
please visit:

kennethdmoore.com
kennydmoore@hotmail.com
@kennydmoore

For more information about
AMBASSADOR INTERNATIONAL
please visit:

www.ambassador-international.com
@AmbassadorIntl
www.facebook.com/AmbassadorIntl

www.ingramcontent.com/pod-product-compliance
Lightning Source LLC
LaVergne TN
LVHW051554070426
835507LV00021B/2574